The Agrarian Crisis in India before Independence

...toward its solution

Revised edition

Written by Rajani Palme Dutt and first published in 1934
With foreword by Professor G. S. Bhalla
Edited and with Introduction by Archana Misra and Kundan Misra

gambol

Gambol Books
SAN: 9028633, ABN: 90 331 674 342
Phone: +61 (0)2 8021 1736, (0)422 251 040
Email: books@gambolbooks.com
Web: www.gambolbooks.com

The National Library of Australia Cataloguing-in-Publication entry

Author:	Dutt, R. Palme (Rajani Palme), 1896-1974.
Title:	The agrarian crisis in India before independence : toward its solution / Rajani Palme Dutt ; editors Kundan Misra, Archana Misra.
Edition:	Rev. ed.
ISBN:	9780980532029 (pbk.)
Notes:	Bibliography.
Subjects:	East India Company--History.
	Agricultural industries--India--History.
	Industrialization--India--History.
	India--History--British occupation, 1765-1947.
	India--Politics and government--1919-1947.
	India--Economic conditions--1918-1947.
Other Authors/Contributors:	Misra, Kundan.
	Misra, Archana, 1980-
Dewey Number:	954.03

Photograph by Luca Peliti.
Reproduced with kind permission from Istituto Nazionale per la Grafica.

Lord and Lady Curzon, hunting the Bengala tiger in the Sunderlands.
The hunt was on the occasion of the durbar of King Edward VII in 1903.

The Agrarian Crisis in India

584   Cooly Woman with her child.

Source: *imagesofasia* © 2009

Postcard from Kolkata 1910

Preface to the Gambol Edition

This book is essentially a reproduction of the original "Agrarian Crisis in India" written by the English Communist Party leader Rajani Palme Dutt, and published in the *India To-Day Series* in 1934.

Despite Dutt's close analysis and poignant argument, the book is difficult to find. We became aware of its existence from a worn copy in the University of Sydney's Fisher Library. While this edition includes a small number of changes in the grammar of Dutt's text, most changes relate to formatting.

As the methods of anti-General Welfare economic policy backed by force used by the British East India Company and, more broadly, the British Empire itself can be seen today throughout the world and in many forms, it was considered worthwhile to re-publish Dutt's pamphlet for today's concerned citizen and citizenry.

Though the proponents and enforcers of the British system are as much its prisoners, at least on an intellectual and moral level, as are those who are outwardly and physically enslaved by it, the obligation remains to shine a spotlight on that system and its methods so that we can readily recognise the operation of that system wherever it survives and the degradation of humanity that results from it.

The education and insights that Dutt provides may prove invaluable for all who wish to act as a force for positive change, and in particular within the framework of a return to the Westphalian era of sovereign nation states working in mutually beneficial concert, with each nation concerned foremost to protect and defend the general welfare of its citizenry, and to allow release of the cognitive, cultural and creative potential of its citizenry.

To a limited degree, Dutt illustrates the connection between these goals, and national development and independence in the agricultural and industrial domains.

Sota Tractors graciously gave permission to use their images, which are presented on the cover and inside the book.

Emeritus Professor G.S. Bhalla in the Centre for the Study of Regional Development in the School of Social Sciences at Jawaharlal Nehru University reviewed the edition and provided critical comments.

Associate Professor Praveen Jha of the Centre for Economic Studies and Planning at Jawaharlal Nehru University also reviewed the edition and returned with feedback. Finally, we thank G. Mythili of the Indira Gandhi Institute of Development Research, Mumbai for commenting on the edition.

Sydney, 2009

Contents

Preface to the Gambol Edition iii

Foreword by Professor G. S. Bhalla vii

Introduction ix

The Agrarian Crisis in India before Independence
...*toward its solution* 1

Author's foreword 5

    India – Britain's slave village   5

    Overcrowding of agriculture   7

    Its effect – poverty   8

    Land hunger   9

    Decline of agriculture   10

    Secret of the growing agrarian crisis   14

Introduction 17

Chapter 1: The land monopoly 19

Chapter 2: Transformation of the land system 27

Chapter 3: Creation of landlordism 31

Chapter 4: Impoverishment of the peasantry 40

Chapter 5: The burden of debt.. 54

Chapter 6: The triple burden... 65

Chapter 7: Growth of the agrarian crisis 71

Chapter 8: Necessity of the agrarian revolution 78

Appendix: British Grid extracts Indian gold 86

Bibliography... 97

Foreword by Professor G. S. Bhalla

Written in 1934, *Agrarian Crisis in India* by Rajani Palme Dutt is a scholarly and incisive analysis of the agricultural economy and the plight of Indian farmers during the great depression.

The basic cause of the agrarian crisis and poverty of the Indian peasantry during the British regime according to Dutt was the *continually intensified over-pressure on primitive small agriculture which, in turn, was the direct consequence of British capitalist policy in India.* First, British policy was instrumental in the de-industrialisation of India which increased the dependence of workforce on agriculture leading to an increasing marginalisation and immiserisation of peasantry.

Second, the British brought about radical changes in land settlements to the detriment of the peasantry. The introduction of Permanent Settlement in the Bengal Presidency in 1891 resulted in large scale conversion of land-owning peasants into tenants and their excessive exploitation by numerous intermediaries. The Ryotwari and Mahalwari settlements introduced later also resulted in the increased revenue exactions through frequent assessments. The result was increasing indebtedness and transfer of land to non-cultivating moneylenders.

According to Dutt, the cultivator was crushed under a triple burden – firstly, increasing demand for land revenue tax, secondly excessive rents in most regions of India, and thirdly increasing indebtedness. The Indian peasantry were thus *faced with urgent problems of existence.*

The immediate solution would have been to reduce land revenue, abolish rents and reduce the debt burden if not eliminate it. *The long term permanent solution lay in reorganising land into cooperatives and collectives for adopting better techniques under large-scale farming. Such reorganisation would, accordingly, have necessarily been part of a wider economic reorganisation, to provide an alternative means of livelihood for the millions inevitably to be displaced from the then-existing agricultural economy, overcrowded as it was. Hence the unity of the tasks of agricultural and industrial development.*

The book has a contemporary relevance since Dutt's prophetic analysis helps to understand the nature of current agrarian crisis in India that has resulted in increasing number of farmers' suicides. More important, the long-term solution suggested for overcoming agrarian crisis holds as true today as at that time.

G.S. Bhalla, Professor Emeritus
(Former Member Planning Commission, Government of India)
Centre for the Study of Regional Development,
School of Social Sciences,
Jawaharlal Nehru University,
New Delhi

Introduction

The crises faced by the world in agricultural and industry are not new, nor are the causes.

This new edition of Dutt's lucid presentation of the causes of the ongoing decline in agricultural output and potential in India as a result of British policies of free trade and financial manipulation can be digested readily by readers in the early 21st century who, the world over, are familiar with – because they are subject to – the same methods.

Equally, the positive and hopeful note of technological development and construction of advanced infrastructure worldwide, within a general welfare-oriented economic architecture, are valid today.

While Dutt wrote from a Marxist perspective, he understood better than Marx the importance to freedom of the human body and mind of the availability of advanced technology and advanced means of production, as opposed to the question merely of who owns the means of production.

Dutt looked forward to a time:

  (a) when Indian agriculture would have access to advanced means of tilling, sowing and harvesting, and

  (b) of indigenous development of such technologies.

Significant progress was made towards (a) during India's green revolution which achieved food independence for India. However, much remains to be done. Through the 1990s and up to the present, it could be said that India strayed from the principles underlying the green revolution as globalisation was embraced. What was lacking during the 1990s and early 21st Century was a continuing mission-oriented focus towards uplifting all parts of India to the degree that, say, Ludhiana Punjab was during the green revolution.

Early in "Agrarian Crisis in India", Dutt makes a point that will surprise early 21st Century readers. Before the British arrived in India, significant strides were being made towards industrialisation with, at least, a significant urbanised artisan class developing. Due to increasing efficiency in agricultural methods, a decreasing proportion of the population was being employed in agricultural activities as the entire nation of India was able to be fed by a shrinking number of increasingly productive farmers. This trend was reversed by the British rulers and their economic methods, forcing a growing percentage into subsistence agrarianism.

India is currently returning to its original industrial tendency, and now with the most modern technology including nuclear power and nuclear desalination. A closed thorium fuel cycle will provide energy independence for India. Much remains to be done.

Water redirection projects are needed, particularly of the Brahmaputra river system, in order to combat the dependence on groundwater.

Better public transport systems are needed, including the introduction of magnetic levitation ("maglev") rail. India would be an important participant in a transcontinental Eurasian-cum-Asian maglev network.

India's space science and for-profit space industry has made strides but, again, even more massive and focussed efforts are needed.

Much work will always remain. Yet today's problems are urgent. The vast majority of India still lives an impoverished agrarian existence. The problem of terrorism persists. The hidden hand behind modern terrorism in South Asia and the illicit drug trade on which terrorism is so reliant is still a dangerous foe of development, of industrialisation and of humanity as a whole. That enemy needs to be targeted so that the axe may be applied to the root of terrorism and drugs, and not merely to their proliferating branches.

In the same vein, by understanding the roots of how the struggling masses of India were led to their current plight, we may derive renewed energy, drive and enthusiasm that these problems have concrete causes and concrete solutions.

There is nothing natural or inevitable about agrarian poverty in India. As Dutt understood the problem in 1934, we can understand it today, and national development forward in great strides. Thus may both courage and hope also be nurtured in the hearts of all those who care not only for India but for all or any part of humanity, and who hold as fundamental the belief that progress and a better future are the right of every human being.

Archana Misra and Kundan Misra, Sydney 2009

The Agrarian Crisis in India before Independence
...toward its solution

Written by Rajani Palme Dutt in 1934
Edited by Archana Misra and Kundan Misra

Herewith we are presenting to the Indian reading public the third number of *The India Today Series*. It is needless to say that this booklet like the previous ones of the Series are reprints from the valuable work of the renowned British Marxist, Rajani Palme Dutt.

– Editor of the Indian Today Series

Author's foreword

India, as we are frequently reminded, especially by those who seem to see hopefully in fact a supposed obstacle to rapid democratic or social development, is a "village Continent".

The contrast between the dependence of the overwhelming majority of the population in India on agriculture and the highly industrialised communities of Western Europe is commonly presented as a kind of natural phenomenon, illustrating the backward character of Indian society and the consequent necessity of extreme caution in proposing changes.

India – Britain's slave village

What is invariably omitted from this vulgar imperialist presentation of the picture is the fact that this extreme, exaggerated, disproportionate and wasteful dependence on agriculture as the sole occupation for three-fourths of the people, is not an inherited characteristic of the old, primitive Indian society surviving into the modern period, but is, on the contrary, in its present scale a modern phenomenon and the direct consequence of imperialist rule. The disproportionate dependence on agriculture has progressively increased under British rule. This is the expression of the destruction of the old balance of industry and agriculture and the relegation of India to the role of an agricultural appendage of imperialism.

The real picture is revealed in the official census returns of the past half-century. The picture would be even more overwhelming if returns of the previous period were available.

436 -- Calcutta. Hooghly River.

Source: imagesofasia © 2009

Postcard from Kolkata 1910: Armed British trade ships

It was during the first three-quarters of the nineteenth century that the main ravages of Indian industry took place, destroying formerly populous industrial centres, driving the population into the villages and destroying equally the livelihood of millions of artisans in the villages. No statistical record of this period is available but the census records of recent decades show that this process has even continued and farther in our time. See Table 1.

Year	Percentage
1891	61.1
1901	66.5
1911	72.2
1921	73.0

Table 1: Percentage of population dependent on agriculture

No. 19 - Astronomical Observatory - Jaipur.

Postcard from India: Astronomical Observatory – Jaipur 1915

That a culture takes the trouble to build an observatory with this degree of sophistication supports the contention it is on a creative trajectory of scientific advancement and industrialisation. This did not suit the free trade-cum-slave system of the British.

Overcrowding of agriculture

Since 1911, this decline of industry, and consequent still further one-sided dependence on agriculture, has reached an even more extreme stage. Between 1911 and 1931 the absolute number of those engaged in industry declined by over 2 millions, while the population increased by 38 millions.

Year	Percentage
1911	5.5
1921	4.9
1931	4.3

Table 2: Percentage of population dependent on industry

While the population during these two decades increased by 12 per cent., the number of those employed in industry decreased by 12 per cent., and this percentage of industrial workers to the total population decreased by more than one-fifth. This reflects the still continuing havoc of "deindustrialisation" – that is, the destruction of the old hand industry, without compensating advance of modern industry, with consequent continuous increase of the overcrowding of agriculture.

Its effect – poverty

But this overcrowding of agriculture, alongside the social conditions of exploitation of the peasantry, is at the root of Indian poverty. The continually intensified over-pressure on primitive small agriculture, which is the direct consequence of British capitalist policy in India, is the basic condition of the poverty of the Indian masses.

The overcrowding of agriculture means that a continuously heavier demand is made on the existing backward agriculture in India to supply a livelihood for an increasingly heavy proportion of a growing population.

On the other hand, the crippling limits of agricultural development under the existing system, owing to the effects of the land monopoly and the paralysing burdens of exploitation placed on the peasantry, make the existing agriculture increasingly incapable of fulfilling this demand.

This is the vicious circle which holds Indian agriculture in its grip and underlies the growing crisis. Its outcome is reflected in stagnation of agricultural development, signs even of deterioration of the existing level of production owing to the excessive burdens placed upon it, and catastrophic worsening of the conditions of the cultivators.

Land hunger

The increasing over-pressure on agriculture means that the proportion of the available cultivated land to each cultivator is continually diminishing.

In 1917 the Bombay Director of Agriculture, Dr. Harold H. Mann published the results of an enquiry in a typical Poona village. He found that the average holding in 1771 was 40 acres. In 1818, it was 17½ acres. In 1820-40 it had fallen to 14 acres, by 1914-15 it was 7 acres. He found that 81 per cent. of the holdings "could not under the most favourable circumstances maintain their owners". And he drew the conclusion:

> "It is evident from this that in the last sixty or seventy years the character of the landholdings has changed. In the pre-British days and in the early days of British rule, the holdings were usually of a fair size, most frequently more than 9 or 10 acres, while individual holdings of less than 2 acres were hardly known. Now the number of holdings is more than doubled, and 81 per cent. of these holdings are under 10 acres in size, while no less than 60 per cent. are less than five acres."

Similar results have been obtained for other provinces.

City	Acres
Bombay	12.2
Punjab	9.2
Central Provinces and Berar	8.5
Burma	5.6

City	Acres
Madras	4.9
Bengal	3.1
Behar and Orissa	3.1
Assam	3.0
United Provinces	2.5

Table 3: Number of cultivated acres per cultivator
as recorded by the 1921 Census

These are average figures in which the extreme shortage of the majority is partially concealed by the larger holdings of the majority.

The Agricultural Commission Report recorded, with regard to cultivators without permanent rights – that is, the majority of cultivators:

> "The Punjab figures, which are the only ones available for a province indicate that 22.5 per cent. of the cultivators cultivate one acre or less; a further 15.4 per cent. cultivate between one and two-and-a-half acres; 17.9 per cent. between five and ten acres. Except for Bombay, which would probably show a very similar result, and Burma which would give higher averages, all other provinces have much smaller average areas per cultivator."

These are facts who significance cannot be escaped. They reveal a desperate, chronic and growing land hunger. They point only in one direction, as similar facts in the agrarian history of Russia pointed.

Decline of agriculture

It is not that there is no cultivable land in India which could not be brought into cultivation. At present only 53% of the cultivable land is under plough. But the extreme poverty of the cultivators, from whom every ounce of surplus and more is extracted, bringing the majority below subsistence level, leaves them completely without resources to accomplish this task. This task can only be accomplished by collective organisation with governmental aid, utilising the surplus resources of the community for this urgently necessary extension of production. But this responsibility has never been recognised by the Government; and it is here that is expressed the signal failure of the existing governmental and social system, which in its earlier period even let fall into complete neglect the public-works and irrigation system maintained by previous governments before British rule, and by its extreme exactions has even driven land out of cultivation, while in the more recent period the beginnings of land reclamation and irrigation works have been fractional in relation to the possibilities and the needs.

But the overcrowded cultivators of India have not only to raise their crops on only 53 per cent. of the cultivable area: even within this limited cultivated area the social conditions, the paralysing burdens placed on the cultivators, their extreme poverty and primitive technique, which they are not left with the resources possibly to develop, mean that, while the demands on the land are heavier than in any other country, owing to the disproportion of the whole economy, the level of production is lower than in any other country.

If we compare the yield of rice and wheat in India with that of China, Japan or the United States, we find the contrast in Table 4.

	India	China	Japan	U.S.A.
Wheat	8.1	9.7	13.5	9.9
Rice	16.5	25.6	30.7	16.8

Table 4: Crop yields per acre in quintals

Source: imagesofasia © 2009

Lack of water infrastructure: This 1915 scene from Jaipur is of a bullock with water-skins and a "bhistee", or water-carrier. A man is squatting to drink straight from the bhistee's water pouch. Bullocks and bhistees served an important role in transporting fresh water to city residents. Residents of desert regions were largely dependent upon bhistees. While some of the population now enjoys a steady supply of water, bhistees can still be found bringing water to the doorsteps of slum dwellers which comprise the majority of residents of many subcontinental towns and cities.

A further comparison is available on the basis of the League of Nation's figures in Table 5.

This contrast is still more marked if taken into relation with the number of workers employed on the land. In India there is one person employed in cultivation for every 2.6 acres of land, as against 17.3 acres in the United Kingdom, and 5.4 acres in Germany. This colossal waste of labour is the reflection of the overcrowding of agriculture and of the low technique.

	Rice	Wheat
India	1,357	652
Japan	2,767	1,508
Egypt	2,356	1,688
U.S.A.	2,112	973
Italy	4,601	1,241
Germany	–	1,740
United Kingdom	–	1,812

Table 5: Crop yields per acre in pounds avoirdupois

This lower yield is not due to natural disadvantages of the lower productivity of the soil. Not only is the existing yield low, but there is evidence of deterioration of productivity. In Bengal it is reported:

"The fertility of the agricultural land is deteriorating steadily on account of the absence of manure. The yield of the different crops has become less and less."

(Bengal Provincial Banking Enquiry Committee Report, 1930, p.21)

Statistics in support of this assertion are given in Table 6.

Quinquennium ending	Wheat	Winter Rice	Gram	Rape and Mustard
1906-07	801	1,234	881	492
1911-12	861	983	881	492
1916-17	698	1,036	867	460
1921-22	688	1,029	826	485
1926-27	721	1,022	811	483
Total decrease:	80	212	70	9

Table 6: Average yield in lbs. per acre in Bengal

Secret of the growing agrarian crisis

Thus from every standpoint, if we examine only the present conditions and tendencies of agricultural production in India in relation to the total economy without yet coming to the growing social contradictions, it is evident that we are faced with a growing crisis of Indian agriculture.

The secret of the growing crisis of Indian agriculture does not lie in any natural disadvantages, nor in any lack of skill and resourcefulness, within the limitations under which they have to work, or supposed innate backwardness of the cultivators, who are thwarted from development, but in the effects of imperialism and the social relations maintained by it, which compel the overburdening stagnation and deterioration of agriculture, condemn the mass of the cultivators to lives of increasing harassment and semi-starvation, and are thus preparing the conditions for a far-reaching revolution as the only outcome and solution. It is to these social relations in agriculture that it is now necessary to turn in order to lay bare the driving forces of the agrarian crisis.

The Author, Rajani Palme Dutt

Source: imagesofasia © 2009

Prisoners making Cane Chairs, Yarrowda Jail, Pune 1910.
Gandhi was held several times during the Independence struggle.

Introduction

"The agrarian system has already collapsed, and the new organisation of society is already inevitable."

Jawaharlal Nehru in 1933.

The crisis of agricultural production, show in the overcrowding, low levels, stagnation and deterioration of agriculture under the present regime, is only the outer expression of an inner crisis of the social relations in agriculture. Under the conditions of imperialism a system of intensive exploitation of the peasantry has developed without parallel in any other country. Within the protective shell of imperialist domination and exploitation has grown up a host of subsidiary parasitism dependent on and integral to the whole system. The resulting process reveals, not only the increasing burdens on the peasantry, their poverty and indebtedness, but the increasing differentiation of classes and the spreading dispossession of the mass of the cultivators from their holdings. The dispossessed cultivators are reduced to a situation close to serfdom or brought down into the ranks of the swelling army of the landless proletariat. This is the process which heralds the approach of future storm.

Chapter 1: The land monopoly

In the traditional land system of India before British rule the land belonged to the peasantry, and the Government received a proportion of the produce. "The soil in India belonged to the tribe or its subdivision – the village community, the clan or the brotherhood settled in the village – and never was considered as the property of the king." (R. Mukerjee, "Land Problems of India," 1933, p.16). "Either in a feudal or an imperial scheme there never was any notion of the ownership of the soil vesting in anybody except the peasantry." (ibid., p. 36).

The "king's share" or proportion payable to the king was traditionally fixed under the Hindu kings at one-sixth to one-twelfth of the produce, though this might be raised in times of war to one-fourth. The Code of Manu laid down:

> "As leech, calf and bee take their food, so must a King draw from his kingdom moderate taxes. A fifth part of the increment of cattle and gold is to be taken by the King, and one-eighth, one-sixth or one-twelfth part of the crops, though a Khastriya King who in time of war taken even one-fourth part of the crops is free from blame if he protects his subjects to the best of his ability."

The Mogul Emperors, when they established their dominion, raised this to one-third. The Statute of Akbar laid down:

> "In former times the Monarchs of Hindustan exacted the sixth of the produce of the land as tribute and tax. One-third part of the produce of medium cultivated land is the revenue settled by His Majesty."

In the period of the break-up of the Mogul Empire, the collectors, to whom the raising of the revenue was farmed out, and who were already elevating themselves to the level of semi-feudal chiefs, and the independent chieftains frequently increased this level of tribute to even as high as one-half.

When the British established their dominion on the ruins of the Mogul Empire, they took over the traditional land basis of revenue; but they transformed its character and they thereby transformed the land system of India.

At the time when they took over, the ruling regime was in decay and disorder; the exactions from the peasantry were extreme and extortionate but the village community system and its traditional relationship to the land were still in the main unbroken, and the tribute was still a proportion (normally in kind, optionally in cash) of the year's produce, not a fixed payment on the basis of land-holding irrespective of the fluctuations of production.

The extortionate tribute of a period of disorder appeared as the starting-point and customary level to the new conquerors. The evidence of contemporary writers indicates that the assessments of the new rulers tended initially to show an increase, or that more efficient collection made the weight of exaction in practice heavier. Dr. Buchanan noted in his "Statistical Survey," conducted on behalf of the [British East India] Company in the early years of the nineteenth century, and constituting the first careful official enquiry, the extremely onerous and even increased character of the new exactions, both in Southern India, surveyed in 1800 and the following years, and in Northern India, surveyed in 1807-14. Thus he wrote with reference to the district of Dinajpore in Bengal:

> "The natives allege that, although they were often squeezed by the Mogul officers, and on all occasion were treated with the utmost contempt, they preferred suffering these evils to the mode that has been adopted of selling their lands when they fall in arrears, which is a practice they cannot endure. Besides, bribery went a great way

on most occasions, and they allege that, bribes included, they did not actually pay one-half of what they do now."

(Dr. Francis Buchanan, "Statistical Survey," Vol. IV, vii, quoted in the Fifth Report of the Select Committee of the House of Commons, 1872.)

Bishop Heber wrote in 1826:

"Neither Native nor European agriculturalist, I think, can thrive at the present rate of taxation. Half the gross produce of the soil is demand by Government. ... In Hindustan (Northern India) I found a general feeling among the King's officers, and I myself was led from some circumstances to agree with them, that the peasantry in the Company's Provinces are on the whole worse off, poorer and more dispirited than the subjects of the Native Provinces; and here in Madras, where the soil is, generally speaking, poor, the difference is said to be still more marked. The fact is, no Native Prince demands the rent which we do.:

(Bishop Heber, "Memoirs and Correspondence," 1830, Vol. II, p.413.)

The historians, Thompson and Garratt, record:

"The history of the pre-Mutiny assessments is a series of unsuccessful efforts to extract an 'economic rent', which was frequently identified with the 'net produce'. The original auctioning of the Bengal revenue farms was an attempt to get as large a share as possible of the 'net produce'. The failure of this system led to the Permanent Settlement. In Madras and Bombay the original assessments were usually based on four-fifths of the estimated 'net produce'. This proved far too high. The first attempt to assess the North West Provinces failed in the same way, and was abandoned in 1832. ... There is no doubt that much suffering was caused, both in Madras and Bombay, by the heavy assessments imposed during the first quarter of the nineteenth century. ... Even in the Punjab, where the British assessments reduced the former Sikh demands, 'it would seem that cash payments and rigidity of collection largely set off the advantage to the cultivator.' (H. Calvert, 'Wealth and Welfare of the Punjab', p.122)."

(Thompson and Garratt,
"Rise and Fulfilment of British Rule in India," p. 427.)

Dr. Harold Mann, in his second survey of a Deccan village in 1921, found a striking contrast between the land (tax) revenue in pre-British days and after British rule:

"A complete change came after the British conquest, when in 1823 an almost unheard of revenue of Rs. 2,121 was collected and village expenses went down to half what they had been in 1817."

(Mann and Kanitkar "Land and Labour in a Deccan Village,"
Vol. II, 1921, p. 38.)

For the thirty years 1844-74 the land assessment for the whole village was Rs. 1,161, or 9 annas 8 pies per acre; for the thirty years 1874-1904 it was Rs. 1,467, or 11 annas 4 pies per acre; in 1915 a new assessment raised it to Rs. 1,581, or 12 annas 2 pies per acre.

Mann and Kanitkar's table of the land revenue assessments, going back to the seventeenth century, is of interest. See Table 7.

In his first survey of a Deccan village, in 1917, Dr. Mann found that the total revenue rose from Rs. 889 in 1829-30 to Rs. 1,115 in 1849-50 and Rs. 1,660 in 1914-15.

In Bengal the land revenue in the last year of the administration of the Mogul's agents, in 1764-65, totalled £ 818,000. In the first year of the East India Company's taking over the financial administration, in 1765-66, it was raised to £ 1,470,000. When the Permanent Settlement was established for Bengal in 1793, the figure was £ 3,091,000.

Year	Land revenue (tax) in Rs	Assessed area in acres
1698	301	1,963
1727	620	2,000
1730	1,173	2,000
1770	1,632	2,008
1785	552	1,954
1790	66	1,954
1803	1,009	1,981
1808	818	1,954
1817	792	1,954
1823 (after British rule)	2,121	2,089
1844-74	1,161	2,089
1874-1904	1,467	2,271
1915	1,581	2,271

Table 7: Increase of land (tax) revenue in an Indian village

The total land revenue raised by the Company stood at £ 4.2 million in 1800-1, and had risen (mainly by increase of territories, but also by increased assessments) to £ 15.3 million in 1857-58, when the Crown took over. Under the Crown the total rose to £ 17.5 million by 1900-1, and £ 20 million by 1911-12. In 1936-37 the figure was £ 23.9 million.

The later figures of land assessment in modern times show a smaller proportion to total produce (the normal basis of calculation being one half of net produce or rent – Mukerjee, "Land Problems of India" p.202) than the earlier figures of the first period of British rule and of the period immediately preceding, the extreme violence of which exactions could not be maintained. But by this time other forms of exploitation had come to play a correspondingly greater part, outweighing the role of direct government land revenue, through the development of landlordism and enhanced rents, commercial penetration, additional taxation of articles of consumption and rising indebtedness. The simple direct tribute of the earlier period, buttressed mainly on land revenue, has given place to the network of forms of exploitation of modern finance-capital, with its host of subsidiary parasites in the Indian economy.

Even so, the level of the assessments for land revenue have shown a continuous tendency also in the modern period to be raised at each revision, with corresponding increased burdens on the peasantry after each revision, leading to movements of revolt. In Bardoli in 1928 a united movement of 87,000 peasants, led by the Congress, successfully resisted an increased assessment and compelled the Government to admit that the revision was unjust and to scale it down.

The angry comment of officialdom on the success of the Bardoli tax strike is significant: the justice of the grievance is not questioned, but the complaint is made that a "precedent" has thereby been set for questioning the justice of all assessments:

> "The assessment of this tract (Bardoli) was revised in the ordinary course; protests against the new revenue-demand were voiced by politicians; and eventually a further official enquiry established, to the satisfaction of the Government of Bombay, the fact that the assessment was altogether excessive. In this case the agitation was justified by the result, but its real significance lies in the establishment of a new precedent. Future re-assessments are likely to become increasingly the subject of political debate."
>
> (W. H. Moreland, C.S.I., C.I.F., "Peasants, Landholders and the State," in "Modern India," 1932, p.166.)

"In Madras, Bombay and the United Provinces, in particular, assessments have gone up by leaps and bounds," writes R. Mukerjee in his "Land Problems of India" (p. 206). He notes that between 1890-91 and 1918-19 land revenue rose from 240 million rupees to 330 million rupees and adds:

> "While the agricultural income during three decades increased by roughly 30, 60 and 23 per cent., the land revenue increased by 57, 22.6 and 15.5 per cent. in the United Provinces, Madras and Bombay respectively. Such a large increase of land revenue coupled with its commutation in cash and its collection at harvest time has worked very unfavourably on the economic position of cultivators of uneconomic holdings, who form the majority in these Provinces" (p. 345).

Chapter 2: Transformation of the land system

Even more important than the actual increase in the burden of the assessments in the initial period was the revolution in the land system effected by the British conquest. The first step in this revolution was in the system of assessments and the registration of the ownership of land, in which English economic and legal conceptions were made to replace, or superimposed on, the entirely different conceptions and institutions of the traditional Indian economy.

The previous traditional "king's share" was a proportion of the year's produce, fluctuating with the year's production, and surrendered as tribute or tax by the peasant joint owners or self-governing village community to the ruler. This was now replaced by the system of fixed money payments, assessed on land, regularly due in cash irrespective of the year's production, in good or bad harvests, and whether more or less of the land was cultivated or not, and in the overwhelming majority of settlements fixed on individual land holders, whether directly cultivators or landlords appointed by the State. This payment was commonly spoken of by the early official administrators and in the early official documents, as "rent," thus revealing that the peasantry had become in fact tenants, whether directly of the State or the State appointed landlords, even though at the same time possessing certain proprietary and traditional rights.

The introduction of the English landlord system (for which there was no previous equivalent in India, the new class being built up on the basis of the previous tax-farmers), of individual land-holding, of mortgage and sale of lands, and of a whole apparatus of English bourgeois legal conceptions alien to Indian economy and administered by an alien bureaucracy which combined in itself, legislative, executive and judicial functions, completed the process. By this transformation the British conquerors' State assumed in practice the ultimate possession of the land, making the peasantry the equivalent of tenants, who could be ejected for failure of payments, or alienating the lands to its own nominees as landlords, who held their titles from the State and could equally be ejected for failure ofpayment. The previous self-governing village community was robbed of its economic functions, as of its administrative role; the great part of the common lands were assigned to individual holders.

In this way the characteristic process of the colonial system was in fact carried out with ruthless completeness in India – the expropriation of the India people from their land, even though this process was partially concealed under an ever-more-complicated maze of legal forms, which after a century and a half has grown into an impenetrable thicket of intermixed systems, tenures, customs and rights, from being owners of the soil, the peasants have become tenants, while simultaneously enjoynig the woes of ownership in respect of mortgages and debts, which have now descended on the majority of their holdings; and with the further development of the process, an increasing proportion have in the past century, and especially in the past half-century, become landless labourers or the new class of the agricultural proletariat, now constituting from one-third to one-half of the agricultural population.

It is to the initial stages of this transformation that Marx makes reference when he stresses the fact that in India the destruction of the ancient village communities was effected, not only by the indirect action of bourgeois commercial penetration and the inroads of machine-manufactured goods, but by the "direct political and economic power" of the English conquerors "as rulers and landlords," and contrasts the much lower process of dissolution in

China "where it is not backed up by any direct political power on the part of the English":

> "The obstacles presented by the internal solidity and articulation of pre-capitalistic modes of production to the corrosive influence of commerce is strikingly shown in the intercourse of the English with India and China. The broad basis of the mode of production is here formed by the unity of small agriculture and domestic industry, to which is added in India the form of communes resting upon common ownership of the land, which, by the way, was likewise the original form for China. In India the English exerted simultaneously their direct political and economic power as rulers and landlords for the purpose of disrupting these small economic organisations."

To which he adds the footnote:

> "If any nation's history, then it is the history of the English management of India which is a string of unsuccessful and really absurd (and in practice infamous) experiments in economics. In Bengal they created a caricature of English landed property on a large scale; in south eastern India a caricature of small allotment property; in the North West they transformed to the utmost of their ability the Indian commune with common ownership of the soil into a caricature of itself."

(Marx, "Capital," Vol. III, xx, pp. 392-3.)

Chapter 3: Creation of landlordism

The introduction of the English landlord system in a modified form was the first type of land settlement attempted by the Western conquerors. This was the character of the famous Permanent Land Settlement of Lord Cornwallis in 1793 for Bengal, Bihar and Orissa, and later extended to parts of North Madras. The existing Zemindars, who were in reality tax farmers, or officials appointed by the previous rulers to collect land revenue on commission (the authorised commission being 2 ½ per cent., though in practice exactions exceeded this), were constituted landlords in perpetuity, subject to a permanent fixed payment to the Government, which was calculated at the time at the rate of ten-elevenths of the existing total payments of the cultivators, the remaining one-eleventh being left for the share of the landlord.

At the time these terms of settlement were very onerous for the Zemindars and the cultivators, and very profitable for the Government. The figure of £ 3 million in Bengal to be raised by the Zemindars for the Government representing a staggering increase on what had been raised under preceding rulers. Many of the old traditional Zemindar families who carried on the old methods of showing some consideration and relaxation for the peasants in times of difficulty, broke down under the burden, and were at once ruthlessly sold out, their estates being put up to auction; there are many pathetic stories of the ruin of this better type of the old Zemindars, who regarded themselves as under some degree of honourable obligation to the peasantry under their care, and found themselves driven out without mercy by the new rulers for failing to raise their quota. A new type of sharks and rapacious business men came forward to take over the estates, who were ready to stick at nothing to extract the last anna from the peasantry in order to pay their quota and fill their own pockets. This was the character of the new "class of gentleman proprietors" which, according to the conceptions of the time, it was the object of the Permanent Settlement to create. In the words of the Report of the Collector of Midnapur in 1802:

> "The system of sales and attachments has in the course of a very few years reduced most of the great Zemindars in Bengal to distress and beggary, and produced a greater change in the landed property of Bengal than has, perhaps, ever happened in the same space of time in any age or country by the mere effect of internal regulations."

Subsequently the system worked the other way, in a direction not originally foreseen by the Government. With the fall in the value of money, and the increase in the amount rack-rented from the peasantry, the Government's share in the spoils, which was permanently fixed at £ 3 million, became relatively smaller and smaller; while the Zemindars' share became larger and larger. Today the total rents in Bengal under the Permanent Settlement are estimated at about £ 12 million, of which one quarter goes to the Government and three-quarters to the Zemindars.[1]

Since this has become clear, the Permanent Settlement is today universally attacked and condemned, not only by the peasantry and the whole Indian people, except the Zemindars, but also by the imperialists; and there is a strong movement for its revision (an example of the violence of the contemporary imperialist attack on

---

[1] The total of rents extracted is increased by illegal exactions. During the Second Session of the Bengal Legislative Assembly, 1937, when the Tenancy Act was under discussion, the total rental of Bengal was assessed by three different speakers at 29 crores (17 crores legal and 12 illegal), 30 crores (20 legal and 10 illegal) and 26 crores (20 legal and 6 illegal). These estimates would represent an aggregate total, including illegal exactions, of some £ 20 million.

---

the Permanent Settlement can be seen in the downright condemnation in the "Oxford History of India," pp. 561-70). The modern apologists of imperialism attempt to offer the explanation that the whole Settlement was an innocent mistake, made through simple ingenuous ignorance of the fact that the Zemindars were not landlords. So Anstey in the standard "Economic Development of India" (p. 98):

> "At first the complicated Indian system was a closed book to the servants of the Company. They began the 'search for the landlord'. ... It subsequently appeared that in most cases these 'Zemindars' had not previously been owners of the land at all. ... At the time they were mistaken for 'landlord' in the English sense."

This fairy tale is plain nonsense. A consultation of the documents of the time makes abundantly clear that Lord Cornwallis and the statesmen concerned were perfectly conscious that they were creating a new class of landlords, and of their purpose in doing it.

The purpose of the permanent Zemindari settlement was to create a new class of landlords after the English model as the social buttress of English rule. It was recognised that, with the small numbers of English holding down a vast population, it was absolutely necessary to establish a social basis for their power through the creation of a new class whose interests, through receiving a subsidiary share in the spoils (one-eleventh, in the original intention), would be bound up with the maintenance of English rule, Lord Cornwallis, in the memorandum in which he defended his policy, made clear that he was explicitly conscious that was creating a new class, and establishing rights which bore no relation to the previous rights of the Zemindars: he was, he stated, "convinced that, failing the claim of right of the Zemindars, it would be necessary for the public good to grant a right of property in the soil to them, or to persons of other descriptions". Sir Richard Temple, in his "Men and Events of My Time in India" (p. 30), records that Lord Cornwallis's Permanent

Settlement was "a measure which was effected to naturalise the landed institutions of England among the natives of Bengal". Lord William Bentinck, Governor-General of India from 1828 to 1835, in an official speech during his term of office described with exemplary clearness the purpose of the Permanent Settlement as a bulwark against revolution:

> "If security was wanting against extensive popular tumult or revolution, I should say that the Permanent Settlement, though a failure in many other respects and in its most important essentials, has this great advantage at least, of having created a vast body of rich landed proprietors deeply interested in the continuance of the British Dominion and having complete command over the mass of the people."

> (Lord William Bentinck, speech on November 8, 1829, reprinted in A. B. Keith, "Speeches and Documents on Indian Policy 1750–1921," Vol. I, p. 215.)

This alliance of British rule with landlordism in India, created largely by its own act, as it main social basis, continues today, and is today involving British rule in inextricable contradictions which are preparing its downfall: along with the downfall of landlordism. While the people of India move forward in the struggle for their independence, in every province the Landholders' Federation, Landowners' Association or the like meets to proclaim its undying devotion to British rule. As typical may be taken the Address of the President of the Bengal Landowners' Association to the Viceroy in 1925:

> "Your Excellency can rely on the ungrudging support and sincere assistance of the landlords."

In 1938 the first All-India Landholders' Conference was held, preparatory to the setting up of an inclusive organisation; and the keynote of the Presidential Address, delivered by the Maharajah of

Mymensingh, was to declare that "if we are to exist as a class" then "it is our duty to strengthen the hands of the Government". In the new Constitution special provision is made for the representation of Landholders, alike in the Provincial Legislative Assemblies and in the Federal Assembly.

But the mistake of the Permanent Settlement was not repeated. The subsequent Zemindari Settlements were made "temporary" – that is, subject to periodical revision to permit of successive raising of the Government's demand.

In the period after the Permanent Settlement an alternative method was attempted in a number of other districts, beginning in Madras. The conception was put forward that the Government should make a direct settlement with the cultivators, not permanent, but temporary or subject to periodical re-assessment, and thus avoid both the disadvantages of the Permanent Settlement, securing the entire spoils itself without needing to share them with intermediaries. This was the Ryotwari system, associated in its institution with the name of Sir Thomas Munro in Madras, who saw in it a closer approach to Indian institutions. This system was advocated by Sir Thomas Munro (at first in a permanent form) in opposition to the Zemindari system already in 1807, and it was put into force by him as a Governor of Madras in 1820 as a general settlement for the greater part of Madras. Its model was subsequently followed in a number of other provinces, and it now covers just over half the area of British India.

The Ryotwari system, although it was advocated as a closer approach to Indian institutions, in point of fact, by its making the settlement with individual cultivators, and by its assessment on the basis of land, not on the proportion of the actual produce, broke right across Indian institutions no less than the Zemindari system. Indeed, the Madras Board of Revenue at the time fought a long and losing battle against it, and urged instead a collective settlement with the village communities, known as a Mauzawari settlement. Their Memorandum of 1818, in which they criticised the Ryotwari method, is worth quoting:

> "Ignorant of the true resources of the newly acquired countries, as of the precise nature of their landed tenures, we find a small band of foreign conquerors no sooner obtaining possession of a vast extent of territory, people by various nations, differing from each other in language, customs and habits, than they attempt what would be called a Herculean task, or rather a visionary project even in the most civilised countries of Europe, of which every statistical information is possessed, and of which the Government are one with people, viz., to fix a land-rent, not on each province, district or country, not each estate or farm, but on every separate field within their dominions.

> "In pursuit of this supposed improvement, we find them unintentionally dissolving the ancient ties, the ancient usages which united the republic of each Hindu village, and by a kind of agrarian law newly assessing and parcelling out the lands which from time immemorial had belonged to the Village Community collectively ... professing to limit their demand to each field, but in fact, by establishing such limit, an unattainable maximum, assessing the Ryot at discretion, and like the Muslim Government which preceded them, binding the Ryot by force to the plough, compelling him to till land acknowledged to be over-assessed, dragging him back to it if he absconded, deferring their demand upon him until his crop came to maturity, then taking from him all that could be obtained, and leaving him nothing but his bullocks and seed grain, nay, perhaps obliged to supply him even with these, in order to renew his melancholy task of cultivating, not for himself, but for them."

(Minute of the Madras Board of Revenue, January 5, 1818.)

This plea of the officers on the spot for a collective settlement and for recognition of "the lands which from time immemorial had belonged to the Village Community collectively" was overborne. The London

Court of Directors decided for Ryotwari system, or in the terms of a document of the time, to "confer the boon of private property" upon the peasantry; and armed with their instructions, Sir Thomas Munro returned from London to impose this system as a general settlement.

Today the forms of land tenure in British India are, in consequence, traditionally classified under these three main groupings, all deriving from the British Government, and reflecting in fact its claim to be paramount landlord.

First, the Permanent Zemindari settlements, in Bengal, Behar and parts of North Madras, cover 19 per cent. of the area.

Second, the Temporary Zemindari settlements, extending over most of the United Provinces, the Central Provinces, parts of Bengal and Bombay, and the Punjab (either with individual or group owners, as in the case of the so-called Joint Village settlements tried in the Punjab), covers 30 per cent. of the area.

Third, the Ryotwari settlements, prevalent in Bombay, in most of Madras, in Berar, Sind, Assam and other parts, cover 51 per cent. of the area.

It should not be supposed from this that landlordism prevails only in 49 per cent. of the area of British India covered by the Zemindari settlements. In practice, through the process of sub-letting, and through the dispossession of the original cultivators by moneylenders and others securing possession of their land, landlordism has spread extensively and at an increasing pace in the Ryotwari areas; the original intention may have been to make the settlements directly with the actual cultivators, but the relations by now have greatly changed. It is estimated that "over 30 per cent. of the lands are not cultivated by the tenants themselves in Madras and Bombay" (Mukerjee, "Land Problems in India," p. 329). In Madras between 1901 and 1921 the number of non-cultivating landowners increased from 19 to 49 per thousand; the number of cultivating landowners decreased from 484 to 381 per thousand; the number of cultivating tenants increased from 151 to 225 per thousand. The Punjab Census Report for 1921 recorded an increase in the number of persons living from rent of agricultural lands from 626,000 in 1911 to 1,008,000 in 1921. In the United Provinces between 1891 and 1921 the number of persons returned as deriving their main income from agricultural rents increased by 46 per cent. In Central Provinces and Berar in the same period the rent-receivers increased by 52 per cent.

The extending chain of landlordism in India, increasing most rapidly in the modern period, is the reflection of the growing dispossession of the peasantry and the invasion of moneyed interests, big and small, which seek investment in this direction, having failed to find effective outlets for investment in productive industry. Over wide areas a fantastic chain of sub-letting has grown up, even to the fiftieth degree. The Simon Report stated, "In some districts, the sub-infeudation has grown to astonishing proportions, as many as fifty or more intermediary interests having been created between the Zemindar at the top and the actual cultivator at the bottom." (Vol. I, p. 340.)

In consequence, much of the tenancy legislation, designed to protect the cultivators, reaches only the inferior landlords, while the majority of the real cultivators, if not already reduced to the position of landless labourers, are unprotected tenants, mercilessly squeezed to maintain a horde of functionless intermediaries above them in addition to the big parasites and the final claims of the Government. This process, carrying the whole system of landlordism to its final absurdity, is one of the sharpest expressions of the developing agrarian crisis in India.

Chapter 4: Impoverishment of the peasantry

The consequent picture of agrarian relations in India is thus one of sharp and growing differentiation of classes.

Role	Number of persons
Non-cultivating proprietors taking rent	4,150,000
Cultivating owners, tenant cultivators	65,495,000
Agricultural labourers	33,523,000

*Table 8: Division of classes in Indian agriculture
as presented by the Census of 1931*

The classification is of only limited value, since the general grouping of "cultivating owners, tenant cultivators" throws no light on the size of holdings, and in consequence makes no distinction between big peasants, middle peasants and poor peasants. In particular, it gives no indication of the size of the majority group of cultivators with uneconomic holdings, whose conditions approximate those of the labourers, and who commonly have to eke out their living as labourers. In practice the margin between the small sub-tenant and the labourer is a shadowy one. To get a truer picture it is therefore necessary to supplement the general Census returns with the results of regional and local enquiries, official and unofficial.

Changes in the system of classification also prevent comparison with previous Census returns. The 1921 Census, by the inclusion of dependents, gave a total for those drawing their living from agricultural cultivation as 221 millions, against 103 millions in the 1931 Census. It is therefore necessary to take the figure of "actual workers" returned in the previous Census, totalling 100 millions, alongside the 103 millions of the 1931 Census, to make even a rough comparison. Even this comparison is vitiated by further changes in the system of classification, through the removal of all those whose agricultural occupation is treated as subsidiary to other occupations and, in particular, through the removal of 7 million women, female relatives of agriculturalists assisting in the work of the farm, to the category of "domestic service," thus giving an illusory apparent effect of a decline in relative proportion of the population engaged in agriculture. This latter change, however, only reinfoces the general effect of the conclusions to be drawn. Table 9 shows a comparison on this basis.

Role	1921 in millions	1931 in millions
Non-cultivating landlords	3.7	4.1
Cultivators (owners or tenants)	74.6	66.5
Agricultural labourers	21.7	33.5

Table 9: Change in agricultural participation from 1921 to 1931

These figures are in detail not comparable, for the reasons explained, especially in relation to the second group. But there is no doubt of the general tendency here revealed, of the growth in the number of non-cultivating landlords (the 1911 figures showed 2.8 millions), and the enormous growth in the number of landless labourers. More detailed figures for Madras are in Table 10.

In the three decades from 1901 to 1931 the number of non-working rent-receivers has increased two-and-a-half times (from 20 to 50 per thousand); this number of cultivating owners or tenants has decreased by one-quarter (from 635 to 510 per thousand); the number of landless labourers has increased from one-third to nearly one-half (345 to 429 per thousand).

Type of participation	1901	1911	1921	1931
Non-working landowners	19	23	49	34
Non-working tenants	1	4	28	16
Working landowners	484	426	381	390
Working tenants	151	207	225	120
Labourers	345	340	317	429

Source: Figures for 1901-21, based on the Census Reports, are given in P. P. Pillai, "Economic Condition in India," p.114; the 1931 figures are taken from the 1931 Census Report of Madras.

Table 10: Agricultural class differentiation in Madras per thousand of agricultural population

Type of participation	1921	1931	Change
Non-cultivating landlords or rent-receivers	390,562	633,834	+61%
Cultivating owners and tenants	9,374,924	6,079,717	-50%
Labourers	1,805,502	2,718,939	+34%

Source: Census returns

Table 11: Bengal change in agricultural participation.

Again the detail figures are not comparable, owing to the change in classification, resulting in an illusory apparent decline of the total agricultural population by 2 millions. But this proves only the more overwhelmingly the actually greater reality of the increase in the proportions of non-cultivating rent-receivers and of landless labourers.

The startling growth in the numbers of non-cultivating rent-receivers has been already noted in the previous section, and is confirmed by all evidence from all parts. This is the reflection of the extending expropriation of the cultivators.

The growth, at the other end of the scale, of the landless agricultural labourers is even more significant. In 1842 Sir Thomas Munro, as Census Commissioner, reported that there were no landless peasants in India (an undoubtedly inaccurate picture, but indicating that the numbers were not considered to require statistical measurement). In 1882 the Census estimated 7½ million "landless day labourers" in agriculture. The 1921 Census returned a total of 21 millions, or one-fifth of those engaged in agriculture. The 1931 Census returned a total of 33 millions, or one-third of those engaged in agriculture. Since then it has been estimated (as in the debates in the Bengal Legislative Assembly on the amendments to the Tenancy Act in 1938; the Madras figures given above also indicate the same) that the real present proportion is nearer one half.

As an aside, consider an enquiry into the conditions of the village of Khirhar in North Bihar in 1939 found that "the most numerous class is that of landless labourers, consisting of 760 families, numbering 5,023 people, forming 72 per cent. of the population of the village". (S. Sarkar, "Economic Conditions of a Village in North Bihar," *Indian Journal of Economics*, July 1939.)

	1842	1852	1862	1872	1911	1922
Field labourer without food (day wage in annas)	1	1½	2	3	4	4 to 6
Price of rice (seer per rupee)	40	30	27	23	15	5

Source: R. Mukerjee, "Land Problems of India," p.222.

Table 12: Wages of agricultural labourers across India

Thus, while the cash wage has increased four to six times in this period, the price of rice has increased eight times – that is to say, the real wage has fallen by one-quarter to one-half during these eighty years of "progress". In the United Province the Report of the Quinquennial Wage Survey in 1934 recorded the average wage as 3 annas or 3d. per day. In 326 villages it was 1½ annas or 1½d. per day.

Descending still farther in the scale, if that were possible, we reach the dark realms of serfdom, forced labour and debt slavery, of landless labourers without wages, existing in all parts of India, about which the statistical returns are silent.

> "On the lowest run of the economic ladder in India stand those permanent agricultural labourers who rarely receive cash and whose conditions vary from absolute to mitigated slavery. Such is the custom of the country in many parts of India that the zemindar, malguzar or ordinary cultivator nearly always contrives to get his servant into his debt, thus obtaining a hold over him which extends even to his posterity.

> "In the Bombay Presidency there are the Dublas and Kolis, who to a greater or lesser extent are bond slaves. Most of their families have been serving for several generations practically as slaves to their masters' households. ...

> "In the south-west of Madras there are the Izhavas, Cherumas, Pulayas and Holiyas, all virtually slaves. On the East Coast the Brahman's hold on the land is strongest and a large proportion of the agricultural labourers are pariahs, who are often Padials. The padial is a species of serf, who has fallen into hereditary dependence on a landowner through debt. ... Such a loan is never repaid, but descends from one generation to another, and the Padials themselves are transferred with the creditor's land when he sells it or dies. ...

> "The lowest depth of serfdom is touched by the Kamias of Bihar, bond servants, who, in return for a loan received, bind

themselves to perform whatever menial services are required of them by their masters in lieu of the interest due on the loan."

(R. Mukerjee, "Land Problems in India," p.225-9.)

In many parts these agricultural serfs and debt slaves are representatives of the aboriginal races. But the position of the former free peasant, who has lost his land and become virtually enslaved to his creditor through debt, or who has been reduced to the bondage of share-cropping, is not far removed from legal serfdom.

Akin to these in many respects is the condition of the plantation slaves, or over 1 million labourers on the great tea, coffee and rubber plantations, owned as to 90 per cent. by European companies, which pay high dividends. The labour for these is recruited from all over India; the workers with their families live on the estates under the complete control of the companies, without the most elementary civil rights; the labour of men, women and children is exploited at low rates; and, although the penal contracts have been formally abolished in recent years and various regulations introduced since the Whitley Report in 1930, the workers remain effectively tied to their masters for prolonged periods, and even in practice in many cases for life.

The pauperisation of the peasantry is shown in the growth of the proportion of landless labourers to one-third or even one-half of the agricultural population. But in fact the situation of the majority of small cultivators on uneconomic holdings, of sub-let tenant and unprotected tenants, is not far removed from that of the agricultural labourers, and the little of distinction between the two is but extremely shadowy. Thus the Report of the Madras Banking Enquiry Committee in 1930 noted:

"We find it difficult to draw a clear line between cultivation by farm servants and sub-letting. Sub-letting is rarely on a money rental. It is commonly on a sharing system, the landlord getting 40 to 60 or even 80 per cent. of the yield and the tenant the rest. The tenant commonly goes on from year to year eking out a precarious living on such terms, borrowing from the landlord, being supplied by him with seed, cattle and implements. The farm servant, on the other hand, uses the landlord's seed, cattle and implements, get advances in cash from time to time or petty requirements, and is paid from the harvest either a lump sum of grain or proportion of the yield. The farm servant may in some cases be paid a little cash as well as a fixed amount of grain. The tenant may cultivate with his own stock and implements, but there is in practice no very clear line between the two; and when the land is an absentee, it is not always obvious whether the actual cultivator is a farm labourer or a sub-tenant."

In 1927 N. M. Joshi, before the All-India Trade Union Congress, estimated 25 millions to be the number of agricultural wage-earners, and 50 millions more to be partly working as wage-earners on the land. Thus the position of the overwhelming majority of Indian cultivators already approximates that of a rural proletariat rather than of small peasant farmers.

In 1930 the Simon Report, that monument of imperialist complacency declared (echoing the Agricultural Commission Report of two years earlier):

> "The typical agriculturalist is still the man who possesses a pair of bullocks and cultivates a few acres, with the assistance of his family and of occasional hired labour."
>
> (Simon Report, Vol. I, p.18.)

How fantastic is this picture in relation to the present realities can already be seen from the facts that have been given. In the evidence before the Agricultural Commission in 1927 an analysis was given of a district of one million acres in Bombat, which was declared to be "infinitely better off than many others". The changes in the

---

proportions of the holdings in only five years between 1917 and 1922 are shown in Table 13.

Holding acreage	Number of holdings in 1917	Number of holdings in 1922	Decrease or increase (per cent.)
Under 5	6,272	6,446	+2.6
5 to 15	17,909	19,130	+6.8
15 to 25	11,908	12,018	+0.9
25 to 100	15,532	15,020	-3.3
100 to 500	1,234	1,117	-9.5
Over 500	20	19	-5.0

Source: Vol. II, Part I of Evidence, p. 292

Table 13: Distribution of agricultural holding sizes in 1917 versus 1922

The witness, a Government official, added in comment:

"These figures referring only to a period of five years appear to me to show a very marked increase in the number of agriculturalists cultivating holdings up to 15 acres, which except in a very few soils is not an area which can economically employ a pair of bullocks. ... There is also a drop in the holdings of 25-100 acres, which means a decrease in the comparatively substantial agriculturalist class who can with luck lay by a little capital."

Thus by 1922 one-half of the peasant holdesr (leaving out of account the army of landless labourers) no longer occupied a holding which could economically employ a pair of bullocks; and this proportion was rapidly increasing.

Any survey of the real situation of the peasantry thus turns on the crucial question of the size of holdings, with regard to which information has been given in the second section of this chapter. The distinction between the "ordinary cultivators", in the old

Census phraseology, whether owners or tenants, and the landless labourers is far less indicative of the real situation than the distinction between the overwhelming majority, constituted by the landless labourers and the cultivators with uneconomic holdings, and the small minority with even economic holdings, let alone the still smaller minority who could be classed as "comparatively substantial agriculturalists" and the non-cultivating rent-receivers.

Here the classic survey of Dr Harold H. Mann on "Life and Labour in a Deccan Village" helps to throw light on the situation. In 1914-15 Dr Mann, who was Director of Agriculture in Bombay, made an exhaustive enquiry into the conditions of a typical village in the Deccan. This enquiry was a purely scientific enquiry into the actual conditions, cultivation, crops, land-holdings, debts and family income and expenditure in a typical "dry" village; but it was the first time that such an enquiry had been fully and exhaustively made. The results were so startling (in the words of the author, so "unexpected" and "depressing") that it was declared in criticism – no other criticism was possible in view of the scientific exactness of the facts – that the conditions of the village in question could not be accepted as typical. Dr Mann thereupon turned his enquiry to another and different village, and in the ensuing study, published in 1921, reached precisely the same results, even more heavily emphasised. Since then, similar surveys in many parts of the country have confirmed the general correctness of these results.

In the first village he found that 81 per cent. of the holdings "could not under the most favourable circumstances maintain their owners". The division of the 156 holdings is given in Table 14.

Size	Number
More than 30 acres	2
20-30 acres	9
10-20 acres	18
5-10 acres	34
1-5 acres	71
Less than 1 acre	22

Table 14: Division of the 156 holdings in village studied by Dr Mann

Following Keating's estimate that "an economic holding of good dry land such as is most in this village in the Western Deccan, and with an Indian ryot's standard of life, would be about 10 to 15 acres," he reached the conclusion that "even if each holding were held in one block, it is evident that a large proportion (81 per cent.) are below this size". This conclusion is reached on the basis of an estimate of the economic minimum for the ryot's standard of life, which touches the lowest level of scanty food and clothing, with no allowance for such a luxury as artificial light. Taking the total of 103 families, he found that those families which were in a "sound economic position" on the basis of their land-holdings numbered 8 out of the 103; those which could maintain their position on the basis of their land by the addition of working outside numbered 28; but those which were in an "unsound" economic position, even on the basis of the fullest earnings from their holding of land and from working outside, numbered 67 or 65 per cent. In the case of the first villagem, however, there was in the neighbourhood a large ammunition factory which provided outside employment for 30 per cent. of the population; and to this extent the conditions were not typical.

In the second village, which was far removed from any manufacturing or industrial centre, 85 per cent. of the families were in this "unsound" economic position. In this village, where the minimum economic holding would be about 20 acres, 77 per cent. of the holdings were below this level. Of the 147 families, 10 were in the first group of being able to maintain a "sound economic position" on the basis of their land-holdings; 12 were in the second of being able to maintain their position on the combined basis of their land and working outside; and 125, or 85 per cent., were in an "unsound" economic position, even on the basis of the fullest earnings from their land and from working outside. This last group included 664 persons out of the total population of 732 – that is 91 per cent. of the population were in this "unsound" economic position.

How do the preponderant majority below this minimum standard eke out a living? They cannot do it. Inevitably they fall deeper and deeper into debt; they lose their land; they pass into the army of landless labourers. The investigation revealed of the ever-tightening grip of debt on the villages. In the first village surveyed the annual debt charges amounted to 2,515 rupees, against a total net return of 8,338 rupees. These debts now form a crushing load amounting to nearly 12 per cent. of the capital value of the village and the actual charges for them amount to 24.5 per cent. of the total profits from land (p.152). The second survey revealed a total charges on debt amounting to 6,755 rupees, against a net return from land of 15,807 rupees, or more than two-fifths of the return from the land were to the moneylender.

Photograph by Luca Peliti, c.between 1890 and 1915
Reproduced with kind permission from Istituto Nazionale per la Grafica.

The pathetic condition of the "natives" of a once-flourishing industrialising nation is shown here as they assist tourists from Italy in the process of crossing a river in northern India. The bear skins were used as floaters. The ladies are the photographer's wife, Giuditta, and her younger sister Milly.

At the end of his survey Dr Mann reached the general conclusion:

> "An average year seems (if our investigations and calculations give anything like a true picture of the village life) to leave the village under-fed, more in debt than ever, and apparently less capable than ever of obtaining with the present population and the present methods of cultivation a real economic independence."

Chapter 5: The burden of debt

As the difficulties of the peasant increase, the burden of debt descends more and more heavily upon him, and in turn increases his difficulties. This is the final vicious circle, which is only broken by the last stage - expropriation. Thus the growth of indebtedness, and of the accompanying processes of mortgaging of lands and of sale and transfer of lands to non-agriculturalists, is one of the sharpest measures of the growth of the agrarian crisis.

"The vast majority of peasants," noted the Simon Report (Vol. I, p.16) "live in debt to the moneylender."

That the burden of indebtedness has grown concomitantly with British rule, and has become an urgent and ever more widespread problem in the most recent period, is universally admitted. Writing in 1911, Sir Edward Maclagan observed:

> "It has long been recognised that indebtedness is no new thing in India. The writings of Munro, Elphinstone and others make it clear that there was much debt even at the beginning of our rule. But it is also acknowledged that the indebtedness has risen considerably during our rule, and more especially during the last half century. The reports received from time to time and the evidence of annual sale and mortgage data show clearly there has been a very considerable increase of debt during the last half century."
>
> (Sir Edward Maclagan in 1911, quoted in the Report of the Central Banking Enquiry Committee, 1931, p.55.)

Already in 1880 the Famine Commission reported:

> "One-third of the landholding classes are deeply and inextricably in debt, and at least an equal proportion are in debt, though not beyond the power of recovering themselves."

Since then this burden of debt has steeply increased. In 1928 the Agricultural Commission reported:

> "It is more than probably that the total rural debt has increased in the present century; whether the proportion it bears to the growing assets of the people has remained at the same level, and whether it has a heavier or lighter burden on the prosperous cultivator than of old, are questions to which the evidence we have received does not provide an answer."

> (Report of the Agricultural Commission, 1928, p.441.)

This fact of the increase was confirmed by the Central Banking Enquiry Committee in 1931:

> "On the question whether the volume of agricultural indebtedness is increasing or decreasing, there is a general consensus of opinion that volumn has been increasing in the course of the last century."

> (Report of the Central Banking Enquiry Committee, 1931, p.55.)

The total volume of rural debt at that time (1931) was estimated by the Committee at 900 crores of rupees, or GBP 675 million. Since then, following the economic crisis and the collapse of agricultural prices, a very steep further increase has taken place, and recent estimates place the total at double that figure (see page 238).

What lies behind this heavy increase of indebtedness under British rule and especially in the modern period? The lighter type of writers, and conventional apologetic treatment, still endeavour to ascribe the indebtedness to the "improvidence" and "extravagance" of the peasantry, and to find the origin of debts in social habits of spending large sums beyond their means on marriages, funerals and similar conventional social ceremonies, or on litigation. Cold facts do not bear out this analysis. Already in 1875 the Deccan Ryots' Commission reported:

"Undue importance has been given to the expenditure on marriage and other festivals. ... The expenditure forms an item of some importance in the debit side of this (ryot's) account, but it rarely appears as the nucleus of his indebtedness."

The Bengal Provincial Banking Enquiry Committee found that, as a result of "intensive village enquiries", the above charge could not be maintained. For example, in the village of Karimpur in the Bogra district, where fifty-two families were indebted, the purposes for which loans were incurred during one year, 1928-29, are in Table 15.

Purpose of debt	Rupees
For repayment of old debts	389
For capital and permanent improvements, including purchase of cattle	1,087
For land revenue (tax) and rent	573
For cultivation	435
For social and religious purposes	150
For litigation	15
For other purposes	66
Total:	2,715

Table 15: Purposes of debt during 1928-29
in Karimpur village in Bogra district

Thus debts incurred for social and religious purposes or for litigation, only comprise one-sixteenth of the whole. Only the second item, covering two-fifths of the whole, could be regarded as in any sense productive debt, representing the lack of capital of the peasant. The remainder, comprising over half, was incurred to meet urgent current needs of land revenue, rent, repayment of debt and current cultivation.

Similar results were obtained in an enquiry in South-West Birbhum, Bengal, in 1993-34. Here out of a total of 426 families in six villages, 234 or 55 per cent., were found to be in debt, to a total of 53,799 rupees, or an average of 230 rupees (£17 5s.) per family. The causes of indebtedness showed the proportions given in Table 16.

Purpose of debt	Rupees	Per cent.
For payment of rent	13,007	24.2
For capital improvement	12,736	23.7
For social and religious purposes	12,021	22.3
For repayment of old debts	4,503	8.4
For cultivation expenses	2,423	4.5
For litigation	708	1.3
For miscellaneous purposes	8,401	15.6

*Source: S. Bose, "A Survey of Rural Indebtedness
in South-West Bribhum, Bengal, in 1933-34,"
Indian Journal of Statistics, September, 1937.*

Table 16: Purposes of debt during 1993-34 over six Bengali villages

The principal item of debt – roughly one-quarter – was incurred for payment of rent; rent and debt together accounted for one-third; rather less than one-quarter went for capital improvement; the proportion for social and religious purposes was higher than in the other example, but still only slightly over one-fifth. The main body of debt was incurred for economic needs, only a minority proportion of this being productive debt.

The causes of the indebtedness of the Indian peasantry are thus economic, and are closely linked with their exploitation through the burdens of land revenue and rent. "The chief cause of indebtedness," in the words of enquiry quoted above, "is the general poverty of the cultivating class". It was Sir T. Hope, a Bombay revenue officer, who declared, in the speech in which he introduced the Deccan Agriculturalists' Relief Bill in 1879, that "to our revenue system must in candour be ascribed some share in the indebtedness of the ryot". "There can be no question," wrote the Report of the Commission of 1892 into the working of the Deccan Agriculturalists' Relief Act, "that the rigidity of the present system is one of the main causes which lead the ryots of the Deccan into fresh debt."

A system which establishes fixed revenue assessments in cash, at a uniform figure for thirty-year periods at a time, irrespective of harvests or economic changes, may appear convenient to the revenue collector or to the Government statesmen computing their budget; but to the countryman, who has to pay the uniform figure from a wildly fluctuating income, it spells ruin in bad years, and inevitably drives him into the hands of the moneylender. Tardy suspensions or remission in extreme conditions may strive to mitigate, but cannot prevent this process. The Commission above quoted collected evidence from a series of villages in the Poona district on how the land revenue is paid. The answers, summarised in Table 17, are illuminating.

"I was perfectly satisfied during my visit to Bombay," writes Vaughan Nash in "The Great Famine," published in 1900, who summarises the above table from the Commission's Report, "that the authorities regarded the moneylender as their mainstay for the payment of revenue."

Village	How the Land Revenue is Paid
Waiwand	Ryots are obliged to pay revenue (tax).
Pimpalgaon	Borrow a little even in good years.
Deulgaon	Borrow in some cases.
Kanagaon	Crops seldom ripen in time for assessment, so ryots have to borrow.
Nandgaon	If rain bad, borrow on security of standing jowar.
Dhond	Borrow on security of standing crops.
Girim	Must borrow on account, or, if no credit, sell standing crops.
Sonwari	Have to borrow to pay revenue, if cannot pay out of savings, or by sale of cattle.
Wadhana	Pay first instalment by borrowing on standing crops. If no crops, mortgage land and sell.
Morgaon	Same.
Ambi	Same.
Tardoli	Pay first instalment by borrowing on standing crops, or, if no crops, borrow on interest.
Kusigaon	Same.

Table 17: How farmers pay their land revenue, according to the farmers

The moneylender and debt are not new phenomena in Indian society. But the role of the moneylender has taken on new proportions and a new significance under capitalist exploitation, and especially in the period of imperialism. Previously, the peasant could only borrow from the moneylender on his personal security, and the trade of the moneylender was hazardous and uncertain; his transactions were in practice subject to the judgement of the village.

Under the old laws the creditor could not seize the land of his debtor. All this was changed under British rule. The British legal system, with the right of distraint on the debtor and the transferability of lands, created a happy hunting ground for the moneylender, and placed behind him all the power of the police and the law, making him an indispensable pivot in the whole system of capitalist exploitation. For the moneylender not only provides the indispensable medium for the collection of land revenue; he commonly combines in his person the role of grain merchant with that of usurer; he holds the monopolist position for purchasing the crops at harvest-time; he often advances the seeds and implements; and the peasants, usually unable to check his accounts of what they have paid and what is due to them, fall more and more under his sway; he becomes the despot of the village.

As the lands fall into the moneylender's hands, the process is carried farther: the peasants become labourers or share-croppers completely working for him, paying over to him as combined rent and interest the greater part of what they produce; he becomes more and more the small capitalist of the Indian economy, employing the peasants as his workers. The anger of the peasants may in the first place turn against the moneylender as their visible tyrant and the apparent author of their woes; the sporadic cases of the murder of the moneylenders even by the peaceful and long-suffering Indian peasants illustrate this process; but they soon find that behind the moneylender stands the whole power of the British Raj. The moneylender is the indispensable power cog, at the point of production, of the entire mechanism of finance-capitalist exploitation.

APPROACH OF GORDON HIGHLANDERS " GUARD OF HONOUR," DELHI, DURBAR.

Source: imagesofasia © 2009

Postcard from Delhi 1903

Source: imagesofasia © 2009

The moneylender was backed by the full power of the state, on display here at the State Entry, Coronation Durbar, Delhi 1911

As the ravages of the moneylenders extend, attempts are made with increasing urgency by the Government, in the interests of exploitation in general, to check him from killing the goose that lays the golden eggs. Volumes of special legislation have been passed for restriction of usurious interest and against alienation of lands. But the failure of this legislation has had to be admitted (see the section of the Agricultural Commission's Report on "Failure of Legislation," pp. 436-7, with reference to the experience of this legislation intended to check rural indebtedness), and is further testified bythe unchecked and even accelerating growth of indebtedness.

The most detailed investigation of the wholeproblem of indebtedness and its growth under rule is to be found in M. L. Darling's "The Punjab Peasant in Prosperity and Debt," originally published in 1925, and in his subsequent books "Rusticus Loquitur" (1930) and "Wisdom and Waste in a Punjab Village" (1934). Despite the generally apologetic outlook of the writer, the facts stand out. In his first work he showed how since the British conquest indebtedness spread in the Punjab.

> "The mortgage that was rare in the days of the Sikh appeared in every village, and by 1878 seven per cent. of the Province was pledged. ...
>
> "By 1880 the unequal fight between the peasant proprietor and the moneylender had ended in a crushing victory for the latter. ... For the next thirty years the moneylender was at his zenith, and multiplied and prospered exceedingly, to such good effect that the number of bankers and moneylenders (including their dependents) increased from 53,263 in 1868 to 193,890 in 1911."
>
> (M. L. Darling, "The Punjab Peasant in Prosperity and Debt," p. 208.)

Mr Darling was of opinion that the moneylender had reached his "zenith" by 1911, and in his evidence to the Agricultural Commission in 1927 he indicated hopefully that "in the Punjab the village moneylender is gradually reducing his business everywhere, except in two districts, and that the main causes of this reduction are the rapid growth of the co-operative movement, the legal protection given to the peasant borrower and the rise of the agriculturalist moneylender" (Report, p.442). But by the time of his next book, "Rusticus Loquitur," published I 1930, despite a general optimistic tone, he had once again to raise the alarm:

> "There is a danger that, despite the land Alienation Act, the expropriation of the peasant may begin again on a large scale. There are already indications of the possibility in the Western Punjab, where the large landlord is taking advantage of the Act to add to his acres at the expense of the peasantry" (p. 326).

By 1935 the Punjab Land Revenue authorities were reporting:

> "The agriculturalist moneylender is apparently gaining strength in the rural areas."
>
> (Report of the Punjab Land Revenue Administration, 1935, p. 6)

In his investigation, made in 1919, Mr Darling found that only 17 per cent. of the proprietors were free of debt, and that the average debt was no less than 463 rupees, or twelve times the amount of the land revenue.

A striking demonstration of the growth of indebtedness is available from the district of Faridpur in Bengal. In 1906 an enquiry was conducted in this district by J. C. Jack, subsequently a Judge of the Calcutta High Court, and its results were afterwards published in his "Economic Life in a Bengal District" (1916); these results showed at that time 55 per cent. of the families in Faridpur still free from debt. A quarter of a century later, in 1933-34, a new investigation was conducted in the same district by the Bengal Board of Economic Enquiry, and it was found that by this date only 16.9 per cent. of the families in Faridpur were free from debt.

Chapter 6: The triple burden

The peasant cultivator, if he has not yet fallen into the ranks of the landless proletariat, thus lives today under a triple burden. Three devourers of surplus press upon him to extract their shares from the meagre returns he is able to obtain with inadequate instruments from his restricted plot or strips of land, even though those returns are already too small for the barest subsistence needs of himself and his family.

The claims of the Government for land revenue fall upon all, as also for such indirect taxation as is able to reach his scanty purchases. Yet the Simon Report laments, "the self-sufficiency of the Indian villages has limited the scope of internal excises to a few articles such as salt, kerosene oil and alcoholic liquors, for which the rural areas are dependent on extraneous supply". Even so, the revenue raised from the duty on salt, the barest need of the poorest, reached no less than £6.6 million in 1936-37, or one-quarter of the land revenue.

The claims of the landlord for rent, additional to the Government land revenue, fall on the majority; since, in addition to the half of the total area of British India under the zemindari system, at least one-third of the holdings in the ryotwari area are sub-let.

The claims of the moneylender for interest fall on the overwhelming majority, possibly, if the figures of Darling and the Faridpur example given above are indicative, as high as four-fifths.

What proportion of the produce of the peasant is thus taken from him? What is left him for his subsistence? No returns are available on his basis question of Indian agriculture. No attempt has even been made to ascertain the total of rent payments additional to land revenue, still less the volume of interest on debt. Failing exact information, the Central Banking Enquiry Committee Minority Report attempted an estimate in the most general terms (pp. 36-7).

Starting from the basis of land revenue at 350 million rupees, this estimate computed the interest on debt as probably, on the most conservative estimate, three times this, or 1,000 millon rupees, and the total or rent, additional to land revenue, as one and a half times land revenue.

This would make a total burden of close on five times the amount of land revenue. Yet this is almost certainly an under-estimate, as this Report indicates. The computation of rent taken by intermediaries as one and a half times land revenue is based on a Bill which was introduced in Madras, and not adopted, to improve conditions by making this a maximum; the real proportion, certainly in Bengal (where gross rental is at least four times and possibly six times land revenue), and probably elsewhere, even though not as disproportionately as in Bengal, is likely to be higher.

The Report inclines to the view that "wherever there are intermediaries, though the condition would vary enormously from place to place and from man to man in view of different kinds of tenure and productivity, the burden on the cultivators would be much greater than is indicated by the proportion 1:1½". The rate of interest on debt, calculated at 1,000 million rupees on a total of 9,000 million rupees, or 11 per cent., is certainly too low; a customary rate with the village moneylender is often 1 anna per rupee per month (sometimes 1½ annas) or 75 per cent. the growth of debt since then to an estimated double of the previous total will have correspondingly increased the burden. The real burden is therefore certainly much heavier than even indicated by this estimate. Yet this estimate would reach a total, if the incidence of the salt tax is included, in the neighbourhood of 2,000 million rupees a year, or 20 rupees per agriculturalist.

Against this we have the estimate of the Central Banking Enquiry Committee Majority Report that "the average income of an agriculturalist in British India does not work out at a higher figure than about 42 rupees or a little over £3 a year" (p. 39).

A closer picture of the rate of exploitation is available fro the detailed "Study of a South Indian Village" by N. S. Subramanian (Congress Political and Economic Studies, No. 2, 1936). The village of Norur is in the district of Trichinopoly, and has a population of 6,200. In this study of the economics of this village the exact budget is presented of the total income of its population from all sources, the total outgoings and the balance available for consumption. The degree of exploitation can here be seen with exceptional clarity, because the land is mainly held by owners outside the village, and the debts are mainly owing to creditors outside the village, so that the bulk of the rent and interest passes out of the village, and presents a clear deduction from the net income of the village.

What are the results that this investigation revealed? The gross income from agriculture, valuing all products at market prices, amounted to Rs. 344,000. The net income from agriculture, after deducting expenses of cultivation (not labour, and excluding wages paid within the village), came to Rs. 212,000. Net income from non-agricultural sources (wages earned outside, salaries of government servants and pensions, interest on capital lent out) came to Rs. 24,000, making a total income from all sources of Rs, 236,000.

Against this, the following outgoings from the village were noted: land revenue, irrigation and allied cesses, Rs. 30,000; rent to owners of land outside, Rs. 70,000; interest on debt (calculated at the lowest rate of 8 per cent.), Rs. 40,000; rentals to Government for toddy and arrack shops, trees taxes, rent to tree owners, Rs. 12,000. This makes a total of Rs. 152,000 for Government revenue, taxation, rent and interest. Together with minor outgoings of Rs. 4,000, the total payments from the village of Rs. 156,000 leave a balance for the village of Rs. 80,000 or under Rs. 13 a head.

It will be seen that each inhabitant of his village earns an income of 38 rupees or £2 17s. for the year. After the tax-collector, landlord and moneylender have taken their share, he is left with under 13 rupees or 19s. to live on for the year. He is left with one-third; two-thirds are taken.

"Of the net total income more than two-thirds goes out of the village by way of land revenue and excise taxes, interest charges and rents to non-resident owners." This is the conclusion reached in this detailed study, which has only been summarised in the above round figures.

Carlyle described the situation of the French peasantry on the eve of the Great Revolution in a famous passage:

> "The widow is gathering nettles for her children's dinner: a perfumed seigneur, delicately lounging in the Oeil de Boeuf has an alchemy whereby he will extract from her the third nettle, and name is Rent and Law."

A more mysterious alchemy has been achieved today in British India. One nettle is left for the peasant while two nettles are gathered from the seigneur.

We end the chapter with the words of Satoki Sharma, landless peasant poet of Muthra District, president of the Village Poets' Conference, Faridabad, May 1938.

"Now awake, brave peasants awake, follow in Krishna's[2] wake.
Thieves and robbers have entered our house. Do not sleep.
Now awake, brave peasants awake, follow in Krishna's wake.
In the month of Baisakh[3] when the peasants reap the crops,
The Bohray[4] confiscate the land and landlords rob the crops.
There is no peace for a day.
They take the fruit of your labour right in front of your eyes,
And leave you not a grain to eat.
Now awake, brave peasants awake, follow in Krishna's wake."

---

[2] Krishna drove Arjun's chariot into the battlefield when Mahabarat was going to be fought. Arjun was diffident to kill his own uncles and relations, but Krishna explained to him the philosophya of war and prepared him for battle.

[3] Month in the Hindu calendar.

[4] Village capitalists.

Chapter 7: Growth of the agrarian crisis

On the basis of the foregoing analysis it is possible to summarise the main features of the growth of the agrarian crisis, whose causes and preceding conditions have been developing through the whole process of British rule and are today gathering to a climax.

The first feature is the increasingly lop-sided and unbalanced situation of agriculture in the national economy, the simultaneous overcrowding and underdevelopment, with still continuing "de-industrialisation," consequent on the colonial position of India. This general situation affects and aggravates all the remaining factors.

The second is stagnation and deterioration of agriculture, the low yields, the waste of labour, the failure to bring into cultivation the culturable areas, the lack of development of the existing cultivated area, and even signs of deterioration of yield, or land passing out of cultivation and of net decrease of the cultivated area.

The third is the increasing land-hunger of the peasantry, the constant diminution in the size of holdings, the spreading of sub-division and fragmentation, and the growth in the proportion of uneconomic holdings until those today constitute the majority of holdings.

The fourth is the extension of landlordism, the multiplication of letting and sub-letting, the rapid growth in the numbers of functionless non-cultivating rent-receivers, and the increasing transfer of land into the hands of these non-cultivating owners.

The fifth is the increasing indebtedness of the cultivators still possession of their holdings, and the astronomic rise of the total of rural debt in the most recent period.

"The waste of labour": use of zero technology, low-energy flux methods such as human muscle is still rife in India.

The sixth is the extension of expropriation of the cultivators, consequent on the growth of indebtedness, and the resulting transfer of land to the moneylenders and speculators, the outcome of which is reflected in the growth of landlordism and of the landless proletariat.

The seventh is the consequent ever more rapid growth of the agricultural proletariat, increasing in the single decade 1921-31 from one-fifth to one-third of the total number of cultivators, and since then developing further to becoming probably one-half of the total number of cultivators.

That expropriation follows on indebtedness is universally admitted. Already in 1892 the Deccan Commission on the working of the Agricultural Relief Act recorded with bitterness "the transfer of the land in an agricultural country to a body of rack-renting aliens, who do nothing for the improvement of the land," and pronounced the new class of landowner to be "probably the least fitted in the world to use the powers of an irresponsible landlord. ... As a landlord he follows the instincts of the usurer, making the hardest terms possible with his tenant, who is also his debtor, and often little better than his slave". In 1928 the Agricultural Commission admitted that the "inevitability of the indebtedness, as it seems to the people, gives the moneylender enormous power. It produces an almost fatalistic acceptance of the steady transfer of land into his possession and leaves his paramount position unchallenged. (p. 435). Incidentally, the virtuous indignation of these Government Commissions against the wickedness of the moneylender land-grabber omits to mention that his power is based on his legal support by the State, including the enforcement of these transfers of land, just as the exactions of Government revenue and taxation first drove the cultivators into his hands. In 1931 the Central Banking Enquiry Committee registered the general conviction that:

"the indebtedness leads ultimately to the transfer of land from the agricultural class to the non-agricultural moneylender leading to the creation of a landless proletariat with a reduced economic status. The result is said to be loss of agricultural efficiency, as the moneylender sub-lets at a rate which leaves the cultivator with a reduced incentive to raise a good crop."

(Report of the Central Banking Enquiry Committee, p. 59.)

The 1931 Census Report reached the conclusion that "it is likely that a concentration of land in the hands of non-cultivating owners is taking place". (Census of India, 1931, Vol. I, Part I, p. 288.)

But this whole process of deterioration, expropriation and increasing class differentiation has been carried very much farther, and very much more rapidly, forward during the last few years as a consequence of the world economic crisis, the collapse of agricultural prices and the following depression.

The extent of the collapse may be seen from the statistics published by the Director-General of Commercial Intelligence and Statistics. In 1928-29, the year before the onset of depression, the value of agricultural crops, taken at an average harvest price, was about Rs. 1, 034 crores. In 1933-34 it was only Rs. 473 crores – a fall of 55 per cent.

The effects of this sudden halving of his income on the plight of the already impoverished cultivator may be imagined. For the money payments he was required to make, he received no corresponding reduction. On the contrary, land revenue, which stood at Rs 33.1 crores in 1928-29, was actually maintained at Rs. 33.0 crores in 1931-32, and had only fallen largely through sheer inability to pay and surrender of lands in many cases, to Rs. 30.0 crores in 1933-34, or a drop of slightly over 9 per cent.

The desperate plight of the cultivators in Bengal can be measured from the estimates given in the Bengal Jute Enquiry Committee Report of 1934, with regard to the variations in purchasing power between 1920-21 and 1932-33. According to these the total value of marketable crops in Bengal fell from an annual average of Rs. 72.4 crores for the decade 1920-21 to 1929-30, to Rs. 32.7 in 1932-33, whereas monetary liabilities actually rose, from Rs. 27.9 to Rs. 28.3 crores. This meant that the "free purchasing power" of the cultivators fell from Rs. 44.5 to Rs. 4.4 crores. The Calcutta Index of Prices fell from an average of 223 to 126 for the same periods, a fall of 44 per cent., whereas "free purchasing power" fell 90 per cent.

It was in this period that the last gold ornaments, the traditional form of savings, were drained from the peasantry to stave off bankruptcy, and served to maintain the annual tribute from India when the export of goods could no longer cover it. Between 1931 and 1937 no less than £241 million of gold was drained from India. But this "distress" gold could only avail a section, and could not serve to put off the evil day for more than a limited period.[5]

In the United Provinces the number of abandonments of land by tenants who could not pay rent reached as high as 71,430 in 1931; the number of orders for the forced collection of land revenue was 256,284. We have already seen how in Bengal in 1930 the

---

[5] For the machinations of Montagu Norman, Governor of the Bank of England, and Winston Churchill which triggered the forced selling by the impoverished Indian population of gold, their final vestiges of wealth, in the quantity of hundreds of tons, see G. C. Preparata *Conjuring Hitler* Pluto Press, 2005. An extract is given in the Appendix.

Committee on Irrigation reported that "land is going out of cultivation".

By 1934-35 the agricultural returns revealed **an absolute drop in the area of cultivated land by over 5 million acres**. In 1933-34 the net area sown with crops was 233.2 million acres. In 1934-35 it was 226.9 million, or a drop of 5,266,000 acres. The drop in the area under food grains was 5,589,000 acres.

The very slight recovery in prices since 1934 has not been able to mitigate the depression or overcome the still continuing effects of the collapse. "Since 1934," writes Anstey ("Economic Development of India", 489 xxvii), "the sufferings of the people may have become more severe."

The burden of debt was doubled by the halving of the cultivators' income. This inevitably meant an increase of debt, which is now estimated to represent a total that is double the level of 1931.

In 1921 the total of agricultural debt was estimated at £400 million (see M. L. Darling, "The Punjab Peasant in Prosperity and Debt").

In 1931 the Central Banking Enquiry Committee Report estimated the total at Rs. 900 crores or £675 million.

In 1937 the first Report of the Agricultural Credit Department of the Reserve Bank of India estimated the total at Rs. 1,800 crores or £1,350 million.

From £400 million to £675 million in the ten years 1921-31. From £675 to £1,350 million in the six years 1931-37. These figures of the mounting total of the peasants' debts during this period give a very sharp expression of the deepening agrarian crisis.

Chapter 8: Necessity of the agrarian revolution

The Indian peasantry are thus faced with very urgent problems of existence, to which they must imperatively find their solution.

Can a solution be found within the conditions of the existing regime, within the existing land system and the rule of imperialism based upon it?

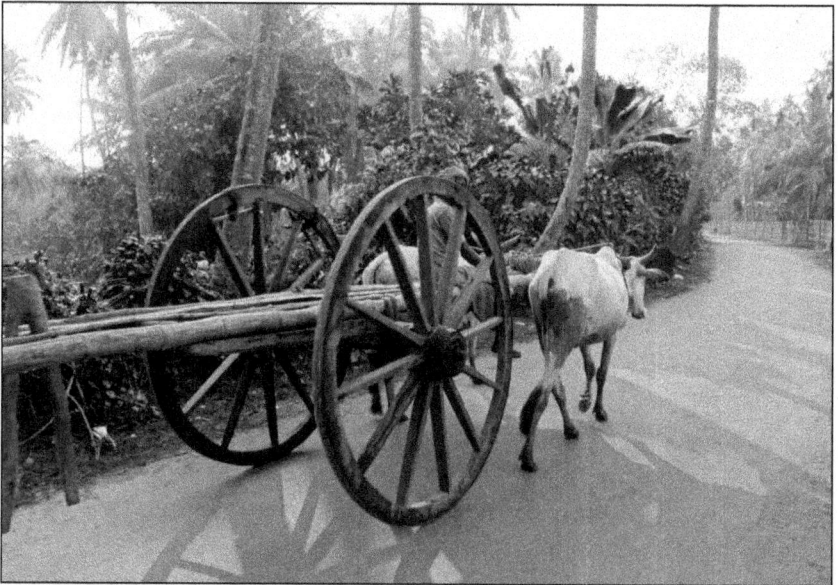

Image licensed

"Far-reaching changes to the technique of agricultural production are essential": Away from bullock power...

It is evident and universally admitted that far-reaching changes are essential, reaching to the whole basis of land tenure and the existing distribution of land, no less than to the technique of agricultural production.

"Far-reaching changes to the technique of agricultural production are essential": ...towards capital-intensive machine methods.

Sooner or later, landlordism must go. In India, as we have seen, landlordism is an artificial creation of foreign rule, seeking to transplant Western institutions, and has no roots in the traditions of the people. In consequence, landlordism is here more completely functionless than in any other country, making no pretence even of fulfilling any necessary role of conservation or development of the land, but, on the contrary, intensifying its misuse and deterioration by short-sighted excessive demands. It is a purely parasitic claim on the peasantry, and most commonly takes the form of absentee landlordism in the case of the bigger estates, with the further burden of additional parasitic intermediaries in the case of the sub-landlords. There is no room for these parasitic claims on the already scant produce of the peasantry. Whatever is produced is required, first, for subsistence, second, for social needs, and third, for the development of agriculture.

The same applies to the moneylender and the mountain of debt. Drastic scaling down and eventual cancellation are inevitable. But this alone would be useless, or only a temporary palliative, unless accompanied by alternative forms of organisation to forestall the cause of indebtedness and supplant the role of the moneylender. This means, in the first place, the removal of excessive demands on the cultivator and the organisation of economic holdings, and, in the second place, the provision of cheap credit, pending collective organisation which would finally replace the need of credit.

It must be recognised that, while partial measures of remission and reduction of rent, and reduction of debt and of the rate of interest, are immediately possible, and were attempted in varying degrees by the Congress Ministries in the Provinces, a more basic approach involves the complete reorganisation of the whole land system. The existence of a large class of some 3 million petty landlords or sub-landlords, very poor themselves, and whose holdings often represent the savings of "old age pension" of low-income urban dwellers, complicates the whole problem of landlordism. In consequence, any temporary measures for the reduction of rent need to be so framed as to ensure that the main incidence falls on the larger landlords. It has been suggested that the method of a graded agricultural income tax (the present income tax does not fall on agricultural income, and thus leaves the landlord immune, while increasing the burden on industry) could effect this object by placing the heaviest rates on the large landlord incomes, while leaving the petty landlords exempt. This, however, while increasing the income of the State, and to that extent, if in the hands of a popular government or Congress Ministry, releasing the potential funds for agricultural development, would not meet the main immediate needs of lightening at once the burdens on the peasantry, unless the funds so obtained were used to reduce land revenue with an accompanying obligatory equivalent reduction of rent. Any more systematic tackling of the evil of landlordism would, accordingly, necessarily be part of a wider economic reorganisation, which would provide alternative means of livelihood for the displaced petty holders, as indeed for the millions who must inevitably be displaced from the existing overcrowded agriculture. Hence the unity of the tasks of agricultural and industrial development.

The essential problem is not only a problem of landlordism, but one of a reorganisation of the whole existing land system and distribution of holdings. A redistribution of holdings is long overdue, both to comat the evil of uneconomic holdings and of fragmentation. When it is recalled that in the Presidency of Bombay, for example, 48 per cent. of the farms comprise less than five acres, and yet total not more than 2.4 per cent. of the entire area (Evidence of the Agricultural Commission, Vol. II, part 1, p. 76), it will be seen how urgent is the need for redistribution. Such redistribution, however, inevitably cutting across a thicket of individual vested interests on behalf of the claims of the majority, could not be accomplished by the bureaucratic action of a foreign government, even if it had the will, but could only be accomplished by the initiative and action of the mass of the peasantry themselves, under the leadership of a government representing them and fighting for their interests.

Redistribution alone, however, can only be the preliminary to tackling the whole problem of agricultural development, raising the technique of agriculture to modern levels, bringing in the use of agricultural machinery, and reclaiming the vast areas of uncultivated culturable land. In this connection it is worth recalling the estimate quoted by the Central Banking Enquiry Committee (Enclosure XIII, p.700) that, if the output per acre were raised to the level of English production, it would mean an immediate increase of wealth by £1,000 million a year, while, if it were raised to the level of Danish wheat production, it would mean an increase of £1,500 million a year (or five times the gross value of agricultural crops in 1933-34, and equivalent to something like doubling the probably actual income of the Indian people). Such an advance, however, would require a decisive break with the traditions of small-scale technique and governmental neglect, and a development, under the conditions of India, towards collective large-scale farming.

The necessity of large-scale farming in order to make possible the use of large-scale machinery is recognised in theory by the experts of imperialism:

> "To begin with prime movers, of which the largest are steam ploughing tackle and the gyro-tiller, the position of such large-scale machinery is clear. They can be employed only on large estates, and even then only where the necessary capital is available. Their work is uniformly good and their use is limited solely by the above conditions. The only possible hope of an expansion in the demand for them rests in cooperative use, which is at present far to seek."

> (Wynne Sayer, of the Imperial Agricultural Research Institute, New Delhi, "Use of Machinery in Agriculture" in the Time Trade & Engineering Supplement, April, 1939).

From the point of view of the expert of imperialism such a development is "far to seek". But the rising social forces of the ruined peasantry and landless agricultural labourers in India are capable of showing in the future period that such a development is not so "far to seek" as these experts imagine. Here the example of the Soviet Union, with its rapid development in two decades, from the poverty-stricken peasantry of Tsarism, through the abolition of landlordism, and after the preliminary stage of redistribution, to the present populous collective farms, is of especial importance for India.

*Photograph reproduced with kind permission
from Sota Tractors – www.sotatractors.com*

Nimble and versatile farm machinery such as shown here ought to be available to all Indian farmers regardless of how small or large their landholding. The Kubota B1502DT 18HP Diesel 4WD with AGMAX Rotary Hoe attached is shown. Such would raise the productivity of the Indian agricultural sector as a whole and, ultimately, contribute to the cultural and cognitive level of the majority of that part of the Indian masses which is now largely engaged in farming. India has the capability to manufacture such or similar machinery in scale, indigenously.

Appendix: British Grid extracts Indian gold

The following is from G. C. Preparata's *Conjuring Hitler* (Pluto Press, 2005).[6]

1st Baron Montagu Norman was Governor of the Bank of England, the British central bank, from 1920 to 1944.

At the right, *Time* magazine 19 Aug 1929 (Vol. XIV, No. 8) presents Montagu Norman.

Hjalmar Schacht (at left), the Economics Minister in the government of Nazi Germany, was positioned in advance by Montagu Norman (at right).

---

[6] Chapter 4: "'Death on the Installment Plan', Whereby Governor Norman Came to Pace the Damnation of Europe, 1924-1933" pp.129-131

A pensive Montagu Norman during one of his many steamship journeys.

Hitler marches out with his Economics Minister, Hjalmar Schacht, behind. Keynesian economist Professor Abba Lerner said in a debate at Queens College New York in 1973 that "Hitler would not have been necessary" had German trade unions accepted Hjalmar Schacht's policies of economic austerity.

The above images could be a springboard for another book. We refer the interested reader to Preparata's book which explains the nexus between the British Empire, the assault – economic and otherwise – on Germany, the genesis of World Wars I and II, and the Nazi Party.

Returning to India, the following lengthy extract from Preparata is included because it illustrates the wider context in which the British Empire's conducted its assault on India and rode the increasingly overworked and underfed shoulders of the Indian peasant.

"Right at the time of Versailles, in June 1919, the United States was experiencing her first post-war boom, an extraordinary credit inflation that had been sparked throughout the world conflict by the massive orders for foodstuffs and supplies on the part of the Allies. Given a plentiful gold reserve, a swelling credit base, surging prices, and low unemployment, America's additional credit-money had set off a feverish stock exchange and real estate speculation, which reached its height in November 1919. The gambling mania on the exchanges drove the rates for 'money on call'[7] to phenomenal heights –20 percent and higher. In London, as in other financial centers, no sooner were such quotes available than balances were drawn from the City, and conveyed along the banking network to Wall Street, to fetch the higher rates. In other terms, capital was exported at once, and as the transfer persisted (British investors selling pounds to purchase dollars), the pound sterling weakened vis-à-vis the dollar, which was the only currency anchored to gold in 1919: to lose versus the dollar was to lose versus gold.

"Considering that the chief objective of Britain after the 'return to normalcy' was indeed to re-anchor her currency to gold, such an escape of capital and the consequential drop of the exchange posed a serious problem. Why was it imperative to re-anchor the currency to gold? 'Prestige!', replied the constables. But that was a lie, and a big one.

---

[7] Loans repayable at the option of the lender or the borrower within a twenty-four hours' notice.

"The Bank was in fact readying herself to plan a game of strategy so complex, and potentially so dangerous that it required the greatest prudence and on the part of the [Anglo-American] clubs privy to its nature. And these knew what mien to deport when it came to parry impudent inquiries from the public into their activities: they simply would 'never explain, never excuse'. A maxim of which 'Norman was inordinately fond'.

"To go back on gold [i.e. the gold standard – Eds], Britain gave herself five years —till the end of 1925. But first, she had to tackle a few problems in her colonies.

"India, whose Grid [Anglo-allied banking establishment] was rather rudimentary, had a proverbial hunger for noble metals, with which debts were settled on an ordinary basis. Her contribution to England's war exertion had been such that, from September 1919 to February 1920, she demanded to be satisfied in gold for her conspicuous trade surplus vis-à-vis the imperial center, thus bringing tremendous pressure to bear upon London. And that, what with the pull from the speculative craze from Wall Street, further enfeebled the sterling. India had tried to secure gold during the war, but she had been sourly rebuffed. She thus had to content herself with either silver or sterling balances.26 Of the latter India wanted no more, and so since gold could not be had from London, she drew on her sterling balances in London to purchase silver from the Americans. But that too, lamented the British Treasury, weakened the pound (versus the dollar). It was time for the financial stewards of the Empire to intervene; and here is what they did.

"They conducted a two-pronged maneuver against their Indian colony. First they struck at the silver market. They unilaterally decreed in 1920 that the silver coinage of England was going to be reduced from a standard of .925 fine to a basic fineness of .500, which is to say that the content of alloy in each silver coin was about to become double of what it used to be. 'Australia, New Zealand and later most of the principal countries of Europe and South America followed suit'. So Britain, withdrew her good (fine) silver coins from circulation and sold them on the markets at the stellar quotes of 1920. The movement brought about immediately a precipitous fall in the price of silver. Thus the steep depreciation of the white metal alleviated the strain exerted on sterling,[8] and in the long run would altogether dispose of one channel through which India imperiled Britain's restocking of gold.

"Simultaneously the stewards assailed the gold front. On February 1920, they decreed unilaterally that the rupee was to be pegged at 2s, two gold shillings. In other words, the British financial officers rendered the rupee enormously expensive in terms of gold, deliberately. The semi-coercive measure was introduced by blandishing India with the deceptive prospect of her buying silver, or anything else she wished around the world, at bargain prices. And so Indian imports, boosted by an artificially strong currency, did boom, while naturally her exports suffered a disastrous decline, which abruptly reversed the trade balance with Britain. Farmers dependent upon exports suffered as they witnessed their prices plummet to match the world level, and as a consequence their income sagged. The final blow was struck by way of the capital account: those absentees in India who could afford to do so, realizing the blatant overvaluation of the rupee and its inevitable fall, moved at once to convert their rupees into pounds, and then convert the pounds into gold. Such capital flight (towards England to buy gold) automatically diminished the gold-standard reserve, which the Indian government maintained in London. To restore this reserve, sterling securities (the standard form of banking collateral), which formed the 'cover'

---

[8] For far fewer pounds were now needed to purchase silver with dollars on the American market; thus the sterling was relieved.

---

of the Indian paper-money circulation, had to be withdrawn from Bombay and remitted to London, and thus, to compensate for the transfer, credit in India had to be restricted.

"Smitten once with an overvalued currency, which by depressing prices struck at their livelihood, and smitten twice with a credit crunch, Indians were at last bereft of any means wherewith to demand gold. Not only that: the Empire's stewards were also shockingly pleased to notice that their scheme had prodded a vast segment of the colony's population to unearth its silver and gold hoards to pay for a debt burden exacerbated by the artificial dearness of the rupee. Indeed, it had caused some gold to come out of the Indian soil, reach the government offices, and ultimately find its way to London in repayment of the adverse balance of payments. By October 1920, India emerged as a net exporter of gold and remained one until the last quarter of 1921. It has been lamented that the Government of India 'was, at best, a mute witness in this sordid affair'.

"Rather devilish than sordid, the tactic succeeded splendidly. The solution was yet provisional, and Norman had had no central part in it, though he must have known every inside detail of the operation, which had begun shortly before he took over at the Bank, and of which, given that India was one of his 'most important financial interests', he impressed a capillary image in his vast memory. Norman certainly had a part, however, and the chief one at that, in the resolution of the first post-war American boom, which truly marked the beginning of his financial regency, and stood as the initial, crucial instance of the stratagems he would have employed a decade later to achieve his, and the Empire's far-reaching goals."

Fast forward to 1931 (G. C. Preparata *Conjuring Hitler* Pluto Press, 2005, pp.185-7):

"But it wasn't over: the Empire's stewards, to make it perfect, achieved this pièce extraordinaire with a solemn finale. Snowden, the chief of the Treasury and 'Norman's devoted slave', in officiating the funeral of the Gold Standard in the House of Commons, appealed with maudlin majesty 'to everyone not to use words...at this moment, which will make things more difficult'. The few skeptics in the House, lest they should crack a 'joke in the cathedral' if they spoke up, kept their mouths shut. On September 23, Norman docked in Liverpool; on the 28th he was back at the Bank. Allegedly, 'he was utterly bowled over on discovering of the terrible truth'. Clearly, Harvey and the others 'had lost their heads'.

"So, here was Montagu Norman, a controversial, and patently ill man in charge of the financial arm of the world's Empire until late July '31 –nine years past the customary term—, who relinquished the command at the most critical juncture of Britain's recent financial history, and in his absence deputized his most delicate duties to a team of semiincompetents. As a result, the Empire's currency fell so steeply as to sever the connection to the gold anchor, and hurl thereafter the world economy down a spiral slide into hell. The Navy mutinied, and upon his return the Governor was pilloried like a monumental loser by a wolfish mob of cartoonists. The pound depreciated by 30 per cent, and the losses of the French and Dutch central banks realized on their sterling balances numbered in the billions of dollars. The outrage of the Hollanders at the double cross was such that they contemplated a legal suit versus the Bank of England; the Dutch Governor, Vissering, was fired on the spot.

"What did the Empire do? Did it fire Norman? Clément Moret, the French Governor, for having held on to his pounds, 'was decorated as a Knight of the British Empire in October'. And Norman was confirmed governor for yet the first of thirteen additional years.

"What of prices and gold? Did prices in Britain, as all feared, shot up because of sterling's fall? No; England, most had seemed to forget, did not suffer the imposition of world prices, but dictated them herself: copper, freights, wheat, cotton, fats, jute, rubber and tin were all quoted on the Empire's markets. It was the others that would have to adjust.

"And Gold? Here is the evolution of the Bank's stocks of the metal between 1925 and 1935 (in million of dollars of 1929 content):

1925	'26	'27	'28	'29	'30	'31	'32	'33	'34	'35
695	720	737	748	710	718	588	583	928	935	973

[We illustrate the Bank of England's gold reserves with the following chart. – Eds]

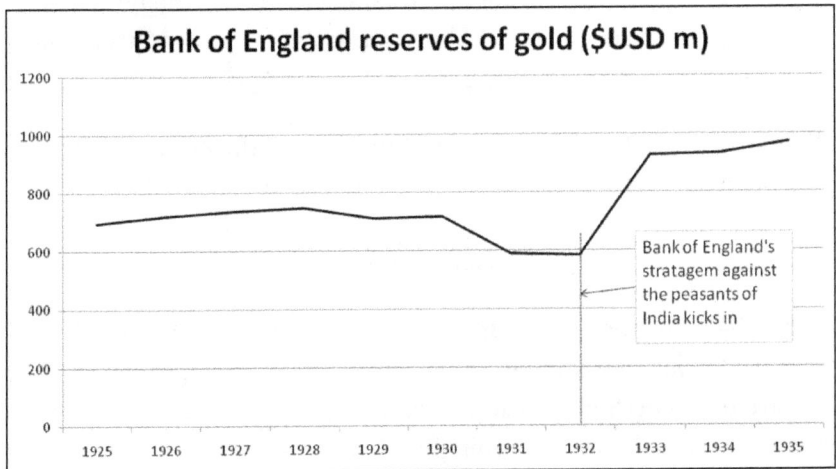

Bank of England reserves of gold ($USD m)

"By late 1932, not only was the gold hoard refurbished, but it had even increased. How? Why, by crushing the Indian serf, of course, with the exact same device employed ten years before. Between 1928 and 1930, the Indian Government was ordered to dump a third of its surplus stocks of silver (90 million ounces), thus causing a diminution in price of the metal of 50 per cent. In 1931, India's Imperial Bank, besieged by the furious protests of India's farmers and merchants, was enjoined to peg the rate at 6 per cent; and even the Bank's director, hand-picked by Norman, remonstrated. The monetary stringency was coupled with a rupee, whose artificial expensiveness in terms of gold, was kept maddeningly high, all of which conspired, in keeping with Norman's expressed wish, to depress local prices and cause a devastating 'money famine'. Despite the turmoil and the fiery indignation of Gandhi, Indians had no alternative but to discharge their debts with the Empire by exhuming their stashes of metal. Which: gold, *sona*, or silver, *chandi*? Since chandi had been rendered nearly worthless, they could only pay England with *sona*. 'Distress sales' they were called. After September 1931, and for the rest of the decade, a torrent of gold welled out of India to irrigate the coffers of the City – the flow was steady and intense. Viceroy Willingdon, ecstatic, reported from the Raj: '...Indians are disgorging gold...'

"September 1931 was indeed 'the watershed of the interwar period'. The British betrayal signaled the 'end of the international financial system established in the 1920s and contributed substantially to the disruption of the international economy.'

"While he had been setting up the Gold Standard, Norman, in view of its forthcoming breakdown, had pulled the sub-Grid of the British Empire together: South Africa, Canada, India, New Zealand and Australia were financially re-engineered, either with the creation of a Bank, or the modernization of the existing one. September 1931 thus found the Empire financially compact, and self-sufficient, with a vast, closed market sheltered by Imperial Preference and soon to be walled by a 20 per cent tariff (October 1932).

"In October 1933, at a dinner hosted by the Lord Mayor at the Mansion House, Winston Churchill lifted a glass to the health of the Governor: 'British banks', he orated, 'have shown themselves capable of a...resourcefulness which has been a definite contributory factor in the strength of the country.'[Cheers]. Norman capped it off with an Arab proverb: 'The dogs may bark but the caravan moves on'."

Bibliography

Bentinck, Lord William, Speech on 8 November 1829 in Keith, A. B. *Speeches and Documents on Indian Policy 1750–1921* vol. I

Bose, S. "A Survey of Rural Indebtedness in South-West Bribhum, Bengal, in 1933-34" *Indian Journal of Statistics* Sept 1937

Buchanan, Dr F. "Statistical Survey," Vol. IV, vii, quoted in the *Fifth Report of the Select Committee of the House of Commons* 1872

Calvert, H. *The wealth and welfare of the Punjab: being some studies in Punjab rural economics* The Civil and Military Gazette Ltd, Lahore 1922

Darling, M. L. *The Punjab Peasant in Prosperity and Debt* Oxford University Press, London 1925

Darling, M. L. *Rusticus Loquitur* Oxford University Press, London 1930

Darling, M. L. *Wisdom and Waste in a Punjab Village* Oxford University Press, London 1934

Bishop Heber "Memoirs and Correspondence" 1830 vol. II

Mann, Dr Harold H. "Life and Labour in a Deccan Village" in *Report of the Agricultural Commission* 1928 (Later published by Oxford University Press)

Mann and Kanitkar *Land and Labour in a Deccan Village* vol. II 1921 (Later published by Oxford University Press)

Marx, K. *Capital* First english edition 1887 Progress Publishers, Moscow, USSR

Moreland, W. H., C.S.I., C.I.F. "Peasants, Landholders and the State" in *Modern India* 1932

Mukerjee, R. <u>Land Problems of India</u> Longmans Green & Co., London 1933

Nash, V. *The Great Famine and its causes* Kegan Paul, London 1900

Pillai, P.P. "Economic Condition in India" George Routledge and Sons, London 1928

Preparata, G.C. *Conjuring Hitler* Pluto Press 2005

Sharma, Satoki (landless peasant poet of Muthra District) *Proceedings of the Village Poets' Conference* Faridabad, May 1938

S. Sarkar "Economic Conditions of a Village in North Bihar" *Indian Journal of Economics* July 1939

Sayer, W. "Use of Machinery in Agriculture" *Time Trade & Engineering Supplement* April 1939

Subramanian, N. S. "Study of a South Indian Village" in *Congress Political and Economic Studies* No. 2, 1936

Thompson, E. and Garratt, G.T. *Rise and Fulfilment of British Rule in India* Central Book Depot, Allahabad 1973

Government reports and other documents

Agricultural Commission, Evidence of the vol. II, 193?

Akbar, Statute of

Bengal Provincial Banking Enquiry Committee Report, Calcutta 1930

Central Banking Enquiry Committee, Report of the, 1931

Central Banking Enquiry Committee Minority Report c.1936

Commercial Intelligence and Statistics, Report of the Director-General of, c.1934

India, Census of Shilong, Assam 1931

Madras Board of Revenue, Minute of the, 5 January 1818

Madras, Census Report of, 1931

Manu, Code of

Smith, V.A. *Oxford History of India, from the earliest times to the end of 1911* Oxford University Press, London 1919

Simon Report vol's I and II, 1930

Punjab Land Revenue Administration, Report of the, 1935

Time Magazine 1929